Someone Other Than a Mother

Someone Other Than a Mother

FLIPPING THE SCRIPTS ON A WOMAN'S PURPOSE AND MAKING MEANING BEYOND MOTHERHOOD

ERIN S. LANE

A TarcherPerigee Book

tarcherperigee

An imprint of Penguin Random House LLC
penguinrandomhouse.com

Copyright © 2022 by Erin S. Lane
Penguin supports copyright. Copyright fuels creativity, encourages diverse
voices, promotes free speech, and creates a vibrant culture. Thank you for
buying an authorized edition of this book and for complying with copyright
laws by not reproducing, scanning, or distributing any part of it in any form
without permission. You are supporting writers and allowing Penguin
to continue to publish books for every reader.

TarcherPerigee with tp colophon is a registered trademark of Penguin
Random House LLC.

Most TarcherPerigee books are available at special quantity discounts for
bulk purchase for sales promotions, premiums, fund-raising, and educational
needs. Special books or book excerpts also can be created to fit specific
needs. For details, write: SpecialMarkets@penguinrandomhouse.com.

ISBN 9780593329313
eBook ISBN 9780593329320

Printed in the United States of America
10   9   8   7   6   5   4   3   2   1

BOOK DESIGN BY KATY RIEGEL

To Janell.

And everyone who trusted me to carry this story,
which is sometimes their story. It was you
who carried me.

Author's Note

WHILE WRITING THIS book, I would wake up in the dead of night sure that I was going to break something. A water glass. Someone's trust. A million little hearts—or three.

So, here is what I did.

For those whose lives intersected with mine through no fault of their own, I have changed identifying details when in the service of protecting their privacy and dignity. Many of these individuals have been kinder to me than necessary. I tried to be likewise.

For those brave souls who consented to an interview, I used audio recordings and e-mail correspondences and sometimes memory to compose and condense their words. Any failing in the accuracy or interpretation of those words is utterly my own. Most chose to use their real names. I am a little in love with them all.

There is a charge in my religious tradition to speak the truth in love. Or, as I prefer to put it, the truth is not a tyrant. May these pages mend more than they break.

We speak as though there is one good plot with one happy outcome, while the myriad forms a life can take flower—and wither—all around us.

—REBECCA SOLNIT[1]

Contents

Preface: Mother or Mother Superior

THERE IS A belief that mother love is a superior love. Like American exceptionalism to which it is closely aligned, the worldview of maternal exceptionalism sees mothers as not just different but better, morally speaking, than those who are not mothers. Mothers are more mature. More selfless. Even more godlike. God is a parent, too, I've been told.

As a young Catholic girl who grew up in the American Midwest on white bread and Jesus, I had two options for a life well-lived: Mother or Mother Superior. I could marry a man and mother my own children, or I could marry God, so to speak, and mother the world's children. Both were good outcomes for someone else's life. Neither would fit the shape of mine.

I was born in the 1980s when motherhood was not, in fact, a given. The widespread legalization of reproductive rights was barely a decade old. Increasing numbers of women were delaying children to pursue an education or career, sometimes opting out or aging out of the traditional milestone altogether. Anxieties about this emerging future fueled conservatives' renewed emphasis on the family and women's distinct place in it.

And what was more distinct about a woman than her womb?

A pious child who picked up on religious rhetoric like it was hopscotch, I was fervently "pro-life"; all children were like hand-knit gifts from God. In elementary school, I wrote a want ad for my future husband that listed "knows the Lord" and "doesn't believe in abortion" alongside must-haves like "loves the outdoors and sports, mainly baseball." But when it came to the idea of my own children, the fervor faded. I wanted to be someone's wife more than I wanted to be someone's parent. More than anything, I think, I wanted to be whoever it was that I was.

It took some time to realize that this would be a problem. *I* would be a problem. At first, I didn't notice that Disney villains were nearly all childless or jealously parenting someone else's children. I didn't catch that relatives started sentences with "When you become a mother . . ." and not "If you become a mother . . ." I almost believed adults who promised with great confidence and zero evidence that my maternal instincts would kick in, despite substandard babysitting skills. But by the time I graduated from college in the South, where tradition hung as heavy as Spanish moss, the message was clear: A woman who embraced a purpose other than parenting was deficient, defiant, possibly devilish—in a word, *cursed*.

It was also clear I had become that woman.

I count it as one of life's dumb blessings that at twenty-two I married a man who was mutually, but not equally, damned. Rush may have been the "head" of our household, as the thinking went among my evangelical friends, but surely I was the controlling "neck" when it came to the question of children. On a blistering summer day in July, we wed in a church ceremony bereft of any blessing for future offspring. No reproductive fruitfulness, please. Or mention of multiplication, thank you, we told our officiants. We were purposefully, prayerfully even, what we would later call "childfree for the common good" and my grandmother would call "interesting."

Community, not parenting, is what compelled us to marry. We thought we were better together; it was as simple and shapeless as that. Like Jesus sending out his disciples, two was enough. But after our wedding day the pressure to start a family, as if we were not already a family unto ourselves, only increased. "You'll change your mind when you get married" was replaced by "You'll change your mind when you get older." The premise felt preposterous to test, as if my body was some high-stakes craps table.

Instead, we began practicing "the ministry of availability" to other people's children. This was not because we liked children per se but because we liked other people and, at a certain age, one has to accept that it's hard to love your grown-ups without learning to love their little ones. "Let us watch your kids so you can go to dinner," I told our friends. "Go grocery shopping. Go to an R-rated movie. Go to sleep." For reasons I can try to explain but change every time that I do, few people called on us. So we called the Department of Social Services, curious if there were parents who might actually need us, if we might actually need them.

Was it possible to do something more meaningful than mothering? You would think that after almost thirty years of childlessness, ten spent coupled and six devoted to earning degrees in gender and theology, the answer would be clear. But the old scripts that said women are made to mother—and made to like it—were legion. Our natural wiring would win out. Our paid work would never pay off. Besides, women are told, "You don't know love until you become a mother."

That last one really fucked with me.

As a THEOLOGICAL anthropologist, or someone who thinks a lot about what humans (*anthropos*) think about God (*theos*), I've spent years talking to people about the stage directions they received on how to be acceptably female. These stage directions are sometimes called social scripts, and they refer to an entire choreography of language, practices, and beliefs that reinforce cultural norms. "Normal" is a community of belonging.

When I first set out to study social scripts, I was hoping to find a universal answer to what made women *women*. I was hoping to find an answer to what made me *me*. I longed for an Easy-Bake manual to my life as much as the next girl. Instead, I discovered that if women are a monolith, it's because we've had to manage some version of the mother scripts* that say our highest self is hiding in our reproductive role. Best wishes, warmest regards, and good luck unlocking your ultimate destiny.

But seriously.

Social scripts are not inherently bad; they're simply the behavioral and conversational shorthand we use to predict, control, and make sense of our mercurial reality. They are ready-made answers to the questions that churn in the night: Why are we this way and not that way? What do we want, and will it make us happy? What does happy feel like exactly? And why do we feel so far from home in these hapless human bodies? The mother scripts take a "typical" woman's body—her womb, her breasts, the anxious heart inside her chest—and promise a way out of the unknowing. A mother's love will always shine a path.

For some lucky souls, this promise pays off. Maybe for a time, maybe for always, motherhood is a revelation. This is true of my own mother, who for most of my childhood was a

---

* There are as many versions of the mother scripts as there are versions of womanhood, which is to say infinite. What follows in this book are the nine that were most alive (and would not die) in my White, cisgender, middle-class, able-bodied, American life.

single mother and worked as little as she could for as much as she could in order to spend as long as she could with my older brother and me. Her only regret is that she didn't have more children. We were that great, apparently.

But for others, the promise of experiencing fulfillment in motherhood is painful, nonsensical, exhausting. I've heard women who don't have children ask, "What's wrong with me?" and women who don't want children moan, "I can't talk to friends anymore," and mothers doing it differently sigh, "I'm tired of having to defend my life."

Along the way, I've learned that the problem with the mother scripts is not simply that they don't work for *some* women. The problem is that they're assumed to work for *all* women, thereby shaming *any* woman who lives beyond their cloud of certainty.

Take, for instance, the script, "Your biological clock is ticking." Are we saying that if you're not worried about your reproductive window or don't feel the pull to parenthood, you're unnatural? Like, maybe your body is a little bit broken?

Or consider the script that says, "Children are a gift from God." It's a lovely belief in the abstract. But I do worry about it being applied individually. Does this mean that if you don't know the blessing of offspring, you're unfortunate? Or, if you don't want the blessing of offspring, you're ungrateful? By this logic, is using contraception ungrateful?

Then there's the script that assures, "But you'd make a great mom!" which is only uttered to some women, the "right" kind of women. The word *mother*, as Alexis Pauline Gumbs has helped me see, is more often a noun that reproduces the status quo than a verb that subverts it.[1]

In some ways, the option for me to make a life as an actual Mother Superior, or regular Catholic nun, was itself subversive. I don't imagine I saw it that way when I was in catechism class. But it did undermine the broadly American notion that biological mothers are the most blessed, their homes the most "missional," their work the most patriotic. So, too, did it undermine the belief that a woman's life should and would center on romantic love, a love born and fueled by feeling rather than the tedium of faithfulness.

Still, even spiritual motherhood can perpetuate the mother scripts. I have a friend in her seventies who knew from a young age that she didn't want children and, in her words, "has wandered that alien path as quietly as possible." Yet every year, she bemoans, people persist in wishing her a happy Mother's Day. "I try to remind them—kindly—that I'm not a mother, and I am corrected, *But you have been like a mother to so many*." What's meant to be a compliment instead feels like coercion. Insisting all women find meaning in our metaphorical reproductive role is no more helpful than insisting we find meaning in our literal one.

Questions of meaning are unavoidably questions of faith. So, how does our faith influence the emphasis we put on mothering? The little evidence that exists on the topic suggests quite a lot. There is quite a lot of correlation between your childbearing attitudes and, say, how literally you read the Bible or how often you attend church or how you religiously affiliate, if at all.[2, 3, 4] It's not surprising then that, across faiths, the religious report more stigma than the nonreligious when deviating from the mother scripts.[5]

Let me be clear here about my own faith. I'm no longer a practicing Catholic, but the prayers still live under my tongue, the incense hibernates in my nostrils. Somewhere in a Las Vegas cathedral, you will still find my father serving communion in a Hawaiian shirt. My mother, on the other hand, attends the same church that I do and talks to God in bed each morning. I talk to God, too, but I have a very wide definition of what this looks like: Breathing can be talking, having a hot cry on the elliptical can be talking, studying scripture can be talking.

I have studied a lot of Christian scripture. So, the story of Jesus is one of the stories I know best, and, on the whole, I think it is a good one for the childless, childfree, and unlikely families.* And yet his followers have caused colossal harm over the last two thousand years by conflating our religious values with popular cultural ones. Even if you're not religious,

---

* A word about words here. While women use different labels (and often no labels) to describe their relationship to children, for the purposes of this book, women who don't have children (for whatever reason) will be identified as *childless*. Within that group, women who don't want children will further be identified as *childfree*. And women who don't center biological children are making *unlikely families*. Honestly, though? Many of us are over the categories completely. But we'll get there . . .

you may have been shaped by Christian idioms regarding everything from the purpose of sex to who counts as family.

"Erin, nobody is thinking about this stuff as much as you," my husband, Rush, once had to tell me.

And I might have left it at that—a writer's tendency to overwork things—had I not noticed how the mother scripts were failing a huge portion of the population. Not just the non-moms they demean. But also the conventional moms they esteem. The titles alone of popular parenting books in the last decade paint a bleak picture. *Fed Up. Maxed Out. All Joy and No Fun.*

And I might have left it at that—a writer's sympathy for other people's misery—had the promise of motherhood not eventually failed me.

ONE YEAR I was childfree, and eighteen months later, I was an adoptive parent of three. Spoiler alert: Parenting was not the shortcut to enlightenment I'd been sold.

In order to be certified as a foster parent in Durham County, North Carolina, you have to take a thirty-hour class on parenting children impacted by trauma. The crew that came together in a room where biology was not destiny and a love life was not the only life was magic. There was a broad-shouldered Black man who wanted better for the youth he pastored. There was a mixed-faith couple who had buried a son and only recently begun to unbury their faces. There was a conservative

White couple whose church took the call to love widow and orphan so seriously that they offered free childcare for anyone who followed the call to this class. How lucky we felt to practice family free from a formula.

In one getting-to-know-you exercise called "the human chain," our first facilitator stood in the middle of the conference room and proclaimed with Oprah-like pitch, "I love pasta!" The invitation was for someone else to stand and say, "I love pasta, too," and join the fledgling circle by linking arms with their new mate. That someone else then offered another benign love to the group—soccer, sewing, cats—and one by one we bound ourselves together by common interests. It was not for lack of effort that I was the last one sitting at the end, but rather firm commitment to the cause. I *liked* but did not *love* soccer, sewing, or cats, and refused to be phony about this or any other loves simply to join the human chain.

Our second facilitator had been the link before me. A more soft-spoken woman, she bobbed her wet, curly bangs left and then right before stopping on a love she thought I—surely anyone—could live with. "I love children," she purred. The blood drained from my face. I willed my bones to stack and rise. Across the circle Rush's cheeks ballooned out and in, out and in. When I finally arrived, I gave her my limp arm and conceded, "I'm getting there."

It was not children in general but children in particular that compelled us to adopt the sibling set of three school-age girls from our first foster placement. "If it had been anyone but you," we still tell them, "we would have quit parenting just as soon as we started." They had hoped to return home to their family of origin. We had hoped they'd be able to do the same. To them, we were a consolation. To everyone else, we were saints.

Suddenly, an outpouring of back pats and attagirls—even thank-yous—appeared from our community, as if to say: *Finally, your life makes sense.* I was now recognizably, irreversibly, a *mom*—a word that came dripping with other people's desire but had little to do with my own. Childfree, my life garnered the blank stare. Mothering, I got the gold star.

I'm not going to pretend I didn't love it at first. It felt good to enjoy the perks of membership in a club I long suspected but couldn't be sure existed. Sermons that turned on parenting tales started to track. Neighbors whom I'd never met appeared with pulled pork and chicken thighs. Friends, as if their lips had been set free, spoke rapidly about their own children. The goodwill was new and bewildering.

But when the shock wore off and the sadness set in, the tender shoots started to push through. Did I want to be celebrated for being a mother? Did I even like mothering, traditionally defined? I started to ask others, "Where's the fanfare for women who are not mothers?" and "Is it okay to not exactly feel like a mom now?" I started to ask God, "Am I just the worst?" and "Make it beautiful anyway, okay?"

What does it look like for an adult woman to love and be

loved as someone other than a mother? It occurred to me that I knew some people whose lives suggested a kind of blueprint.* This is the story of how I used their stories, along with a small dumpster of research, to make peace with my story.

ANOTHER WAY OF saying the same thing: This is a book about making meaning beyond motherhood.

I have practiced making meaning beyond motherhood in two life stages now: one as a person intentionally without children and one as a person suddenly raising three. I don't presume that these dual experiences are shared by many. Mine is a strange confluence, and I like it that way, mostly. Not belonging can give you the ability to see something from the outside, to see something other than sides.

From this vantage, I can see that there are gobs of us who are making meaning beyond motherhood, whether we come to it as a mom, a non-mom, or someone in between. We want a purpose bigger than body parts. We want an identity fuller than children (lack of or love for). We want a legacy larger than our own kin. We do not want to be seen as more mature or immature, selfless or selfish, holy or unholy, than anyone else solely on the basis of our parenting status. Most of all,

---

* In case you are wondering, I found these people in my friend circle and my writing circle and my local church circle. While we represent different ages, races, gender identities, and physical abilities, we all have a college education and a roof over our head. This is one of the book's (many) limits. But it's also one of the book's (many) invitations. Pay attention. Start close in. These women may be nearer to you than you think.

I think, we want to have conversations with each other in which the edges are not so sharp.

The circumstances that led me to go looking for meaning beyond motherhood were largely chosen (painstakingly so), but it need not be this way for everyone. You may go looking out of curiosity or boredom, you may be on the fence: Do I want to be a mother, and if not a mother, then what? How could that be a good life, too? Or perhaps it is some grief—a diagnosis, divorce, motherhood itself—that causes you to listen for a new story, a kinder story, about who you are when you are not the woman you thought you'd be. Sometimes you go looking when time grows long, nothing dramatic about it, except that you didn't plan to be here, and now here you are, and you would like to make sense of how things turned out without turning to resentment. Increasingly, you go looking because you have no choice. You have to reckon with the singular, astonishing life you have.

This book is about what happens when that life is not the same as the life you expected, the life expected for you, to be acceptably female.

So, here is what we will do. We will set out to investigate the old scripts and, along the way, test out some new ones. Getting rid of the scripts altogether may appeal to the most committed anarchists among us. But I am inclined to believe that in the absence of good alternatives the traditional scripts only grow bigger teeth. Each chapter is my attempt to offer you one good alternative. The pattern might sound familiar:

You've heard it said that it is like this. But I am suggesting to you that it is like that.

My story provides the scaffolding to the book, but the real aim is to invite you to consider the movements of your own life. (I like movements better than parts; movements suggest something more cyclical, edgeless.) The first movement is a snapshot of me discerning a purpose without children, without biological children. This is who I know myself to be. Why does it feel not okay to be this way? Can God use this, me? I want to be useful but not used up. We try fostering.

In the second movement, I am fashioning a life in which the word *woman* is not synonymous with the word *mother*. You can be a woman who does not identify as a mother. You can mother without also being a biological parent. You can enjoy non-procreative sex. What does this look like? Does this require a lot of energy? My energy is dissolving; I am in the weeds of parenting.

Finally, there is the life-in-review movement. Some things have happened, some things remain. It's not so much *Should I?* or *Shouldn't I?* anymore, but *How do I understand this life?* Are there regrets? What is legacy? Am I different? There were days, especially around the time of the adoption, that I grieved no longer being childfree. I still grieve aspects of no longer being childfree. This grief feels honest, healthy even.

But what I no longer grieve is a loss of identity. You know, the idea that I was once that kind of person and now I am this kind of person. More and more, I think that I am the same person. (This is less depressing than it sounds.) I am the same person who knows some things now, not because I am a mother but because I am a grown-up. To be a grown-up is to know the joy and limits of writing your own story, within some bigger stories.

I wish I could report that it's easy to rewrite the mother scripts. It's not; it ruins perfectly decent conversations, requires long explanatory texts. Whether you are single or coupled, infertile or ambivalent, stepparent or biological parent, it gets exhausting all the same. To feel out of sync with friends. To hear the same tired lines from family. To wonder if something's broken on the inside. Still, if I can assure you—and, on dark days, me—of only one thing, it's this: It's worth it to labor for a world in which the capacity to love and be loved is not limited to those with the "mom gene."

If there is such a thing.*[6]

---

* The jury's still out. Researchers discovered a so-called "mom gene" in mice, but no definitive human parallel has been found to indicate which women are "born" to mother or which women will be any "good" at it. Thanks be to God.

Discerning a Life Well-Lived

CHAPTER 1

Script: Your Biological Clock Is Ticking

Rewrite: The Sound of Your Genuine Is Calling

*There is in every person something that waits
and listens for the sound of the genuine in herself.*
—Howard Thurman[1]

DEEP IN THE heat of 2018, I am in my home in Raleigh, North Carolina, sitting at the dining room table, interrogating one of my best friends about mothering. Or, in her case, not mothering. I'm hoping she can help me make sense of something strange.

It's been a little over a year since I legally became a parent after decades of being childfree. This isn't even the strangest part, although I'm having a terrible time trying to explain myself to myself. The strangest part about becoming a parent has been the reaction from my community. Elation. Relief. Recognition. One friend expressed shock—"Holy shit. Okay then."—when I shared the news, but nearly everyone else responded as if motherhood was not only the most exciting thing I'd ever done but also inevitable. "I knew you'd come around to having children," my aunt confessed, "even if you had to do it unconventionally."

It's possible that a large part of the fervor was precisely because Rush and I had come to parenting unconventionally. Our people, which is to say White, Christian, American people, do love a good adoption story. We are nothing if not optimistic about the salvific power of family. Still, while it may be highly praised, it is not highly practiced. "Bless you," the church ladies would say to me in one breath, followed by, "I could never do what you did," in the next.

To be fair to all our enthusiasts, most women do end their childbearing years with children of some kind. But I have not "come around" to being one of them. I can still hardly call myself a *mom*, though I do understand that this is a widely agreed-upon word for a female parent. There are good reasons for my resistance. One, the girls already have a woman whom they call *Mami*, and neither they nor I are interested in replacing her. Two, I never really intended on becoming a mom, so while I've been researching the role for some years, I've had scant time to make it my own. (That I want to make it my own—as precious and unique as an individual snowflake—is, I'll give you, a very modern dilemma.) And three, I am keen to believe that a woman doesn't have to be a mom in order to be Someone.

It must be said, *or people will worry*, that I care deeply for the three small Someones—hereafter referred to as Oldest, Middle, and Youngest—under my roof. I care deeply that they are safe and supported and capable of penning a hand-written thank-you note when the occasion calls for it. Hours of my life are given to scheming what helps each of them to be a human person. Is it a beautiful book? A sewing class? A different parenting strategy? Giving up on the strategies entirely for a while? There is little I like more than sitting shoulder to shoulder with a child while we order personal hygiene products from Target.

So, I am doing the work of loving and living for more than myself, even if I, like many parents, do not enjoy it half the time. This is not my main trouble with motherhood. My main trouble is that I thought I was doing this work, albeit with different people, before I became a mother, and I do not fully get why people are so galvanized by my life now. Or what was so uninspiring about my life before.

A life before motherhood has historically and stereotypically been cast as a prepubescent version of what it could be. Nothing wrong with it, in theory, but to try and stay there forever would be to enact, in the words of C. S. Lewis, "a perpetual springtime."[2] It would be small-minded, underdeveloped, and not just a little bit narcissistic. A perpetual springtime would also be highly *unnatural* anywhere but San Francisco.

And so, I've taken it upon myself to start sitting down with friends, especially friends not mothering, or not mothering traditionally, and grabbing them by the proverbial hands to say, "Motherhood is not inevitable. Finding your purpose in motherhood is not inevitable. You are not inevitable." In other words, I want to tell them what I wish someone had told me.

More to the point, I want to know how I might embrace my life as a parent without dismissing my life as a nonparent. Contentment, I've gathered, can be a good look. Contentment *with* conviction.

Hence, I've set off in the doldrums of a Southern summer to begin, and I know exactly the woman I want to begin with.

Paying Attention to What Makes Us Tick (And What Doesn't)

Janell looks resplendent in the sunlight streaming through my book-lined dining room. Her blue eyes are wide and unflinching. A topknot of long brown hair sits fat and happy on her head. Every so often, I swear her nose ring actually twinkles. Mind you, the afternoon light is also highlighting a week's worth of kid crumbs ground into our thick, wool rug.

The truth is the trappings of my life, my home, have changed some since I first met Janell. Rush and I were living in a different house, just twenty miles up the highway in Durham, when she arrived on our patio carrying a bottle of molasses whiskey and a grin almost as big. We fell fast for one another. The second time we met, she spent the night in our guest room. It was still a guest room then, outfitted in Ikea white. The drapes were white. The dresser was white. The carpet was *mostly* white. There was no place to put a suitcase.

Was that barely five years ago?

Janell has arrived with no suitcase today. Although she's lived in Denver, Colorado, for most of our friendship, she travels through town often for her work as a trained facilitator. We're both trained facilitators, actually. (Is it so very hard to make an agenda? she texts me. No, it is not, I text back.) She leads suicide prevention programs for middle and high school students. When I'm not writing, I lead retreats for people exploring questions of purpose. Questions of purpose are the best kinds of questions in our professional opinion and yet they often go unasked, assumed.

This is especially true of life paths that are culturally prized. A woman has a vision for a wedding and the frothy tulle dress, without asking if she wants a marriage. A woman has a vision for a pregnancy, now with the clever announcements and gender reveals and nurseries painted in trendy tricorn black, without asking if she wants a child.

We get hung up on the trappings of a life and miss the deep desire of a life.

Which is why I'm staring Janell down across my dining room table now. She is skilled at attending to her life, and I am confused about mine, or is it others who are confused? This is my point. I don't know. To some observers, our lives have diverged. She is a single woman without children. I am a married parent of three. She describes herself as a person with "child-freedom"; I have started referring to my life as "childfull."

So, Janell and I are different. I know that. In some ways her life is the one I used to have, and I want the record to show that it was a good one. But I also want to recover something of my purpose now. How does one do this? What gets in the way? This is what I intend to find out.

"I need to get the language right," I begin.

"Of course you do," she concedes.

"You don't call yourself *childfree*. But *child-freedom*. What's that?" I pause, taking a sip of bubbly water, the unofficial drink of thirtysomething-year-old women.

"Right. Well, I really respond to the word *freedom*. I was at a yoga class earlier this week when a lovely man named Tony offered the mantra 'I name my needs with joy and freedom.' And my whole body lit up." She balls her hands up into tiny fists and then explodes them like fireworks to illustrate.

"Thank you for that," I nod.

She laughs. "So, because I've not dedicated myself to tiny humans exclusively, *child-freedom* is a celebration of my ability to move through the world quickly and creatively, without any plans but with lots of extended eye contact and undistracted presence."

I want Janell to tell me more about this child-freedom given that I've been missing mine here in this full house. Tell me more about what it looks like to be a *soul* before a *role*. Remind me what it feels like to not necessarily be free *from* children but free *for* myself.

A forester had once explained the asexually reproducing spider lilies to me similarly. *If they don't need pollinators, what are they for then?* a man had inquired on our urban hike. I expected our guide to say that they were for our viewing pleasure. But then she said something even more pleasing than that. *What are they for?* she repeated. *They are for themselves.*

"So, would you say you came into your child-freedom by chance, choice, or calling?" I have promised cupcakes later if she can endure this somewhat formal interview for a Friday afternoon.

Janell snickers, sending a ripple of energy through her bare shoulders, and says, "Well, it's like a spicy little cocktail of those things—and potentially more."

For starters, she tells me, at thirty-six years old she's never been in physical proximity to someone with whom she wants to make a baby. But she's also never ached to create space for a baby to grow. "I've done an internal check a number of times through the course of my life," she says to me, "and I haven't ever gone inside and found that pulsing, sort of heartwarming, or more like a heartbeat, for mothering a child of my own."

"So, you're not concerned about your biological clock?" I blurt out, not because I'm concerned, but because this is a concern other people have expressed to me.

Once, at a party, a single woman I'd only just met shared, unsolicited, that her inner alarm had gone off suddenly. Now she was frantic to know how she could come by a biological child. "I'm not sure," I offered helplessly, "but that must be frightening."

Then there was Rush, home from a vasectomy consultation and reporting that the doctor was worried. "Worried about what?" I asked. "Worried about what my future, younger wife might want if you die," Rush explained. Oh. How thoughtful.

Look, I have no problem admitting that women face fertility constraints as we age. Personally, I am looking forward to being postmenopausal. In a soliloquy from the television show *Fleabag*, Kristin Scott Thomas rants, "Yes, your entire pelvic floor crumbles and you get fucking hot, and no one cares, but then you're free, no longer a slave, no longer a machine with parts. You're just a person."

Now, really, I don't believe anybody is a machine with parts. But that does seem to be the big idea behind the biological clock, doesn't it? For a good portion of our lives, women's bodies are seen as baby-making machines. It's not just what they were designed to do but what they want to do. Our window for having children is inevitable. Our craving for having children is inevitable. Our future is inevitable.

Wasn't that the whole point of my dear aunt's comments? I had finally succumbed to the great inevitability, even if I had sidestepped the whole giving birth part.

But are our bodies really that scripted? As far as Janell knows, she's not yet heard the clamor of any clock. She leans out of the afternoon light, bites her lip, and sighs. "My only concern is that mine is broken."

"Broken, how? Like, what if it goes off after it's too late?" I ask.

"No, broken, like, what if it never goes off at all?"

Watching shadow wax over her pale face, I wonder how many other women have felt this same way. Defective. Like they were missing some important factory setting. Or belonged on the island of misfit toys. It is incomprehensible to me that Janell has ever worried about being broken, given my obscene admiration for her, and yet aren't I sitting here, hiding behind the guise of an interview, only slightly worried about the same?

LATER, I WILL do some rooting around.

It turns out that when the idea of the biological clock was first introduced in 1927 by an American biologist named Curtis Paul Richter, it was used to argue that animals are largely shaped by learned rather than instinctual behavior.[3] We're talking biorhythms here, not bio-drives. Think, for example, about how your body responds to jet lag. You typically get up around seven o'clock in Raleigh. But when you visit your brother in Seattle, you rouse at more like four- or five-ish. Gradually, if you stay for more than a few days, your body adjusts to the time change. Your "biological clock" recalibrates to its environment. Even if the human body is "a machine with parts," Richter's work was among the first to suggest that it was a highly adaptable one.

Not until an article appeared in the *Washington Post* in 1978 was the concept of the biological clock reportedly first linked to a woman's fertility.[4] In the piece titled "The Clock Is Ticking for the Career Woman," columnist Richard Cohen reports how he'd been going around from woman to woman, asking, "This business about the biological clock? How do you feel about it?" (Already he's using the term inventively by asking only women and providing answers only about babies.) While some said that the biological clock meant nothing—they could always adopt if the mood struck—most, he reported, felt resentful of a reproductive deadline, resigned that the desire would materialize whether they liked it or not, or bothered by the difference between their fertility window and men's. What compelled Cohen to be such a busy bee isn't made clear until the end of the piece. No matter the great strides for women's rights in the last decade, he wrote, "There was something about their situation that showed, more or less, that this is where liberation ends."

So that was it then. The biological clock was no longer a fact of life but a tool of oppression. Women were bound to want children, and supposedly, men didn't have to worry about it.

For the record, I do not find any evidence for a natural yearning to make babies in women. (An evolutionary yearning, though? I suppose you could say we have one as a species, but there's still no across-the-board desire in individuals for their genes to survive. Human beings are complicated like that.) Sociologist William Goode once summed it up this way: "There is no innate drive for children. Otherwise, the enormous cultural pressures that are there to reproduce would not exist. There are no cultural pressures to sell you on getting your hand out of the fire."[5]

So "no" to scientifically stimulated urges to procreate. But "yes" to socially stimulated ones. In fact, in one study I came across, researchers documented the onset of so-called "baby fever" in both men and women.[6] And it didn't correlate to biological triggers or signals. Instead, it was the exposure to other people's babies that illuminated one's desire for a child and, if present, could amplify that desire to a feverish pitch.

THAT'S WHAT'S SO striking to me about women like Janell. When it comes to discerning the question of whether or not to bear a child, sometimes it's the silence within that's loudest.

I ask other friends about what it's like not to feel the mythical ache. Iris, a coupled thirty-two-year-old, thought the urge to grow a baby would kick in when she entered a healthy, committed relationship; it hasn't yet. Lisa, a single forty-one-year-old pastor, sits on the mourner's bench with people who weep when they are not able to get pregnant and realizes she's never bumped into that feeling. "I've let that be a teacher for me," she says. After watching her niece and nephews for the weekend, Margaret, thirty-eight years old and divorced, is beginning to discern that it isn't that she's incapable of caregiving, only that she may not want to when the energy required is so total.

And, still, the world spins.

So, the biological clock as we commonly know it is a myth. I decide this is good news for everyone. It means there's nothing broken—or superhuman—about women who don't want children. But it also means there's nothing weird—or embarrassing—about feeling the pull to parenthood. Quite the opposite. If the clock is not real, not ravaging women of all sense and agency, then those who *do* want children aren't possessed. They can have the dignity of owning their desires. Sure, these desires may feel sudden, inexplicable, uncool even. But a woman needn't dismiss herself by chalking them up to what writer Gabrielle Moss calls "dumb lady brain."[7]

We can each take ourselves seriously, each honor our body's (many) mysteries, and each pay attention to what makes us tick—and what doesn't.

The Thing Behind the Thing

Allow me to share something that will not shock you: I, too, have never heard a clock go off in the dark of my woman parts. But how do you know? How do you know that you don't want children—or perhaps, that you want something more than children? Truthfully? I don't know how *you* know. But I can tell you how *I* knew. Or, rather, how I began to know.

When I was a child, I had a Cabbage Patch doll named Alicia. She came everywhere with me in the collapsible stroller I'd push around our Chicago suburb. We'd scooch into a booth at Pizza Hut, and I'd request a high chair for her. We'd barrel into our minivan, and I'd tuck her tummy fat under the seat belt. She even went on family vacations with me; pictures show us sitting side by side on an airplane with silk eye masks on—one for me, one for her.

On the day of my First Communion ceremony at Our Lady of Humility Catholic Church, Alicia sat in the first pew as I made a meal out of Jesus Christ, the God who became man and made his body food for the world. So eager was I for a taste of this good life that I begged to receive the sacrament two years earlier than my older brother, Charlie, had. Already a theologian-in-training, I loved my tradition too much to believe it couldn't make room for me.

It was around this same time that my mother, a woman we call Perky Patty or "Perk" for short, showed me my first birthing video. Perk was a registered nurse on the mother and baby unit then, all goofy glasses and fluffy hair and scrubs with bears holding balloons. Stories trailed her home from the hospital—how she calmed an anxious mom who was learning to breastfeed or got mouthy with a doctor who didn't push enough pain meds.

I'm not sure she showed me the birthing video, as much as the tape was rolling in the den as I rolled in, but it was one of those can't-look-but-can't-*not*-look moments. The image of a woman's vagina stretched wide and foaming at the mouth with something green—why was it green?—is one I wouldn't forget. A tetanus shot was my version of terrible then, and I could not imagine willingly welcoming more. If I clung to an early belief in the miracle of life, it was swiftly paired with the bodily reality.

The message that stuck? Giving birth was serious work, and I should give it serious thought. This worked out well, given my bent toward serious thought.

After the Birthing Video Bomb of 1989, it wasn't so much that I counted myself out of conceiving. It was that there were so many other breadcrumbs worth following. I wanted to be a soap opera star who commuted from the New Jersey suburbs, or a travel agent who worked in a cubicle with a watercooler. I wanted to live a hundred lives; it seemed slipshod to choose a path for which I had little curiosity.

Slowly, my imagination grew as the templates for a woman's life grew with me. In elementary school, Alicia was joined by somewhere between eighteen to twenty-two dolls who regularly sat around the perimeter of my sponge-painted bedroom. Upright. Open-eyed. Ready for instruction. With my allowance, I bought used textbooks from school rummage sales and handed them out to each student, being careful to assign the bigger books to the bigger bodies.

We even celebrated picture day. I still have as evidence a

faded album in which a photo of each doll appears accompanied by a slip of paper with his or her full name on it. *Sean Michael. Kayla Lynn. Hope Kristen.* These names were a portal to another world, a universe I could birth with my own words.

In the end, I played with dolls much longer than I thought tenable and eventually gave them up much easier than I thought possible—to Goodwill, to neighbors, to a nose-picking younger cousin. Not one lives somewhere in a box with my name on it.

So, why am I telling you all this?

I look back on my childhood now and think how easy, easy but sloppy, it would have been to assume this love of dolls prophesied a love of children—and an aspiration to raise them. But behavior is not the same as desire. Practice is not the same thing as purpose. To discern the latter, I had to get curious about the thing behind the thing. And I did not want to raise dolls.

I wanted to collect them like ideas.

I wanted to organize them like stories.

I wanted to name them like their lives were titles to books only I could write.

Dolls offered one more important clue to my existence, and it was a clue that seemed to me both blessing and curse: I felt most myself by myself.

So, more than the infamous room of one's own, I was beginning to think a quiet womb sounded quite right, too.

When Procreation Doesn't Equal Purpose

Were such grand plans even allowed?

It did not occur to me until I was much older that the God-man I adored had no biological children of his own. In catechism class, when I received my first WWJD bracelet meant to remind teens to consider "What would Jesus do?" childlessness was left off the list of attributes worth imitating, unless of course you wished to do so through lifelong abstinence. According to the Catholic Church, procreation was pretty much God's "grand plan" for humanity, like it or not.

"So do you ever draw on your faith tradition to support your child-freedom?" I ask Janell, back in my book-lined dining room. Rows of serious-colored theology tomes, stacked neatly on floating shelves, suggested I had done a lot of "drawing on" over the years.

At this, she looks at me as if I have asked the equivalent of "Do you ever draw on fifth-grade math to make sense of the mole on your shoulder?" It is not a question she has considered. "Support? No," she says, followed by a long pause, then a conciliatory, "I don't think so." She tries to explain.

"The evangelical container I grew up in didn't allow me to imagine that the childfree life could be a gift or a goodness," she reflects, pulling her knees up to her chest. "Even now, when I talk about not wanting to mother, I'm sort of shopping it around like a test balloon of sorts and only in very calm weather systems outside my hometown."

This news is startling to me. Janell has always been, in my mind, the Patron Saint of Self-Love. But if my private library has taught me anything, it's that it's tricky for women who grew up religious to test out alternatives to the mother scripts. (When I ask, Janell can think of no adult in her childhood who wasn't either parenting on purpose or infertile.) After all, we were likely to hear that God intends for us, desires for us, or commands for us to procreate.

So, while scientists have been unable to prove a natural imperative for bearing children (aside from the evolutionary one), many of us are aware of the religious imperative: "Be fruitful and multiply."

WHATEVER YOUR SPIRITUAL persuasion, you may have heard the story: God makes humankind in God's image and tells them to fill the earth.

A literal reading of this story might assume it's about the universal command to procreate. Men and women are meant to make love and make babies so that the world is full of God's people. Not only are these instructions considered good sense for the continuation of the human race, but also for the continuation of the faith. We know, after all, what happens to religious sects like the Shakers, who some two hundred years ago organized into celibate families. Two converts remain in a lovely little village in Maine.

But there's another reading that suggests the story isn't so much about a command but a blessing. I found the explanation in one of my favorite theology tomes. You see, if "be fruitful and multiply" were uttered only to the first humans (and the winged and sea monsters, too), then a literal interpretation might be perfectly logical. There is an empty earth and a need to fill it. However, the divine decree to "be fruitful" is issued again, to two more recipients, both men, and men who have already procreated at that.*

Why does it matter? Well, to start, it makes little sense to command someone to do what they've already done. And second, men weren't considered the ones responsible for reproductive matters in the ancient world. They were responsible for political matters. Women's omission from the blessing suggests it doesn't concern individual baby-making. It concerns collective nation-making. Procreation is useful but ultimately secondary to this end.

Further, it's worth pointing out that more often than not, the God of the Bible does not say "be fruitful" but "I will

---

* If you are nerdy and curious, the men who receive the blessing are Noah (and his three sons) and Jacob (already the father of twelve). Noah was an obvious recipient. After a worldwide flood, there was a new need to fill the earth. Jacob may have been a symbolic recipient. Just before Jacob receives the blessing, God renames him Israel, again, suggesting that nation-making is the goal rather than baby-making. Some people also include Abraham in the list of initial recipients. But God does not tell Abraham to "be fruitful." God instead says, "I will make you exceedingly fruitful." The emphasis is on what God will do, not what humans should do. *Should* is a sticky word.

make thee fruitful," causing some scholars to suppose that those of us who come after are fulfillments of a promise rather than its foot soldiers.[8] It was settled then, right? I could assure Janell that modern folk are not mandated to multiply—literally, individually, everlastingly—at all.

Not quite.

"Be fruitful and multiply" is often only half of the religious imperative. The other half is what's called natural theology, or the belief that bodies, bent as they are toward God's likeness, can be read like maps for divine intention. If women have wombs, God intends for us to use them. If women can bear children, God intends for us to want to. I could do exegetical gymnastics all day, and someone will still point to my reproductive organs as proof enough that I was made to mother. It doesn't matter what the Bible has to say; it just *makes sense*, they will say.

This is a little scary to me, given that the grandees of Western thought once thought a woman's womb, in the words of Plato, so "possessed with desire to make children that it careened through the body and attached itself to other vital organs, causing all varieties of disease."[9] In another troubling speculation, the patriarchs of early fertility religions professed women who ovulated on the full moon were on the "good mother cycle," in sync as they were with the earth's fecundity, whereas women who ovulated on the new moon were cast as witches, sirens, or wisewomen, their most fertile time of the month "wasted" in the days of darkness.[10]

My point is that humans, being human, have had a lot of theories about how bodies, and desires for that matter, work. Both might be from God, but they could also be tremendously vexing.

Neither are as legible as fifth-grade math.

So, HOW DO we make out what we're made for?

The word *calling* is one Janell's been noodling with more and more recently. In spiritual traditions, we often think of what's being called, invoked, or named as one's higher purpose or God-given purpose. In modern contexts, the word has gained in popularity as more and more people expect and long for a purpose both grand and singular. That's no small hope, especially when bodies fail and relationships beg and money looms.

After graduating from college, the financial reality of being a writer forced me to explore another thing other than the writing thing. (True story: I once received a royalty check for seventeen cents.) So, I moved to San Francisco to work in book publishing. I met an author named Parker Palmer who was training folks to lead retreats on vocational discernment. I imagined my thing could be helping others find their thing.

It was while working as a retreat facilitator that I began to name this thread as a curiosity about how we know we know. How can any of us know what we're supposed to do with our lives, let alone an afternoon? Instead of using human nature to read God's intentions, I became more compelled by the opposite. How do the cosmic stories we believe shape our own sense of purpose?

My hundred-year-old windows now steaming with condensation behind her, Janell lays her purpose out for me like a puzzle. "I can remember being young and wanting to adopt, like, a hundred babies. And then Angelina Jolie did it sometime when I was in high school, and I thought, *Oh, no. That doesn't ring true.* But it seemed to make sense at the time because that was my context for understanding how someone with my impulses could do my work in the world. Parenting was presented almost as the exclusive option—or not even an option at all."

Janell didn't dream of making humans, though. She dreamed of doing humanitarian work. And for a while she did just that, first moving to Liberia to work with women and girls impacted by the civil war, then doing community development for an underserved neighborhood in Philadelphia. After taking a year off to rest and reset, she signed on to her current job in which she campaigns for resilience and wellness in school cultures.

Still, her tender through line—her thing behind the thing—continues.

"I'm not doing humanitarian work with like systems or structures anymore, but I do feel like I'm doing humanitarian work on a one-to-one basis. Like, broken heart because of a boy? I'm coming to be where you are for the next few days.

Broken heart because of your children? Come hang out with me and I will be delighted to talk with you and walk with you and you can drink Diet Cokes and I'll not because I'm off the sauce." Janell takes a deep breath, loosens her topknot, and straightens her spine. "So that does feel like a response to a calling. It just looks very different than I had imagined."

I know what she means.

And it occurs to me that I, too, have become a member of her broken hearts club, since I began parenting. Except now I'm beginning to think I'm not broken so much as breaking open, which is another way to say that I am grieving the life I planned to be present to the one I have. The one in which three girls will spill through the front door soon. The one in which a guest room now doubles as Oldest's bedroom, and a gallery of posters featuring kittens in oversized shoes.

"So, do you ever grieve, you know"—I rest my hands on my belly—"not doing the procreation thing?"

Janell leans forward and rests her elbows on the table, pushing her cheeks up into a lazy grin. "As I explore my mature body, I do wonder what pregnancy or childbirth would feel like. Like, how might my body shift and expand to bring new life into the world? I think I would have made a great surrogate." She throws her head back and laughs. "But then I remember I'm already doing that. I'm already expanding to bring new life into myself, my relationships, my narratives. So, I'm fine. I'm not sad about it. And I'm not mad about it."

She goes on, "Instead, this is a result of some discernment that I did in my life when I took a fierce inventory of who I am and how I feel and what I want in me and in the world. And the conclusion that I drew is I won't mother in this one specific way. And look. Look at how much capacity I have. Look at how big my life and heart have become in that." Her eyes are shiny with tears as she finishes, the strands around her face as wild as the spider lily's in the afternoon glow.

"Well, I think you are a freaking sign and wonder," I tell her, pushing my chair back for cupcakes as promised.

"Thank you." She sighs, adding, "I mean, I've made jokes about my scrambled eggs but only because I'm fitting in with a cultural narrative about what my eggs are for."

This is, I think to myself, precisely the trouble with the script about the reproductive biological clock, or the literal reading of "be fruitful and multiply": The authority on a woman's worth, a woman's purpose, lives only and always outside of herself. Biology becomes destiny. Discernment traded for inevitability.

Janell had called it a fierce inventory, this attempt to turn from mindlessness to mindfulness and trust that there is also a galaxy of wisdom within. Various cosmic stories call this internal source of authority the true self, the inner teacher, the Holy Spirit, and on and on it goes. (I call her "Love," as in "Hi, Love" or "Help, Love.")

It doesn't matter what you call it, Parker used to tell me,

but that you call it something. Why? Because to not call upon its wisdom is to go numb. It's to want only what others want you to want. It's to settle for the trappings of a life instead of the beautiful absurdity of life itself.

Humanity Is the Great Inevitability

So, this is the something strange Janell has helped me make sense of: Motherhood is not inevitable. Our humanity—our hungry, baffling, glorious humanity—is the great inevitability. We are not machines (or maps); we're a song.

In his 1980 baccalaureate address at Spelman College, Dr. Howard Thurman assigned the newly minted graduates only one task: to pay attention to your deep desire. He called this desire "the sound of the genuine," and at the heart of his message was the belief that every person ought to spend their days getting still enough to listen for "their unique and essential idiom."[11] To recognize the notes of your life so you don't end up humming the chords to someone else's.

I have often used this speech in my work as a retreat facilitator, assuming it was a poetic answer to the very American question, "What do you want to be when you grow up?" And what you wanted mattered. And what you wanted could be trusted.

So, I might have gone on believing if I had not, after Janell's late-summer visit, returned to my handout of Thurman's words. I read it again, this time finding an added bit at the end that I've never given much attention. The revelation sends me swiveling in my cheap office chair.

Thurman took a guess at what the sound of the genuine might sound like, and to my surprise, it had nothing to do with what you wanted to do for a living or even how you hoped to make a family. No matter that you might want to become a "doctor, lawyer, or housewife," he said to the fidgety young women before him.

Instead, he said, your deep desire sounds more like this: "I want to feel that I am thoroughly and completely understood." Or this: "I want to feel completely vulnerable, completely naked, completely exposed and absolutely secure." After a few days of meditating on it, by which I mean typing and deleting and retyping, I think mine sounds like this: "I want to be free, free *and* full, free to hold the fullness of worlds within me."

Put simply, the sound of the genuine is that in you which is "irreducible" to body parts or even life paths. It is the desire in you where human and divine are thought to coincide.

Much of the excitement about my adopting children seemed to assume that it marked an inevitable shift in my desire, a welcome departure from prepubescent fantasies. And it's true, the external shape of my life, and home, has changed irrevocably.

But now I'm beginning to suspect that this shift has been a

little, well, overdramatized. That the internal shape of my life is still very much recognizable. That mothering is not, in fact, an about-face from my irreducible desire to be free—free and full—but simply one possible outcome of it.

One stupefying outcome.

CHAPTER 2

Script: Home Is Your Highest Duty

Rewrite: Desire and Duty Can Share a Roof

*It seems impossible that desire
can sometimes transform into devotion;
but this has happened.*
—ALICE WALKER[1]

WHEN I SET out to rewrite my life, I had hoped to avoid
the puzzling part about how I got here and focus on the more
practical matter of what to make of things now. After reread-
ing Thurman's words, this is proving impossible. Apparently,
I need to go deeper than my wish *not* to become a mother. I
need to go back farther than all this blessed breaking open. I
need to remember how it is that my body did not become a
home for someone else.

My home became a body, a container in which life could
grow.

SO, THIS IS where our story begins again: spring 2012, Durham. The trees were already dressed in their sticky cardboard

belts to prevent the annual climb of cankerworms when our neighbors Kevin and Emma moved in with us. Emma was eight months pregnant.

It was the first home Rush and I had ever owned. We had moved from a motel-style apartment crawling with fleas and trumpet flowers in Oakland, California. The first time I did laundry in the quiet of my own hallway, I cried. No quarters required. No nasty notes about the etiquette of moving someone's wet clothes. Here, in this three-bed, two-bath, 1,400-square-foot bungalow, everything was under my thumb.

My immediate family was tickled for me. My older brother, Charlie, sent a postcard pounded out on his typewriter, the only anything I allowed pinned to the fridge for years: "New houses are like blank postcards. Overwhelming at first, but sooo fun once you get the juices flowing." Perk told me not to worry. I could always sell if I panicked. Nothing is permanent. Dad said not to wait on all the projects; do them now and love where you live.

Which I thought was funny coming from him. After the divorce, every house he lived in was furnished with boxes. Mostly file boxes. Sometimes wardrobe boxes. Once, I shoveled boxes of single-serving ramen noodles out of the backseat of his Subaru so we had enough seats for everyone, by which I mean Rush, who sat with his arms wrapped around his shins for two hours while my dad wound his way home from California wine country.

Perk's houses, on the other hand, were organized into

piles. Growing up, I used to walk around turning piles of pens parallel to one another and squaring off pads of paper, only to come back through and find my work undone. I wouldn't call her messy so much as hospitable to the clutter. She never met a bobblehead that couldn't be grafted into our home. It was the same with people. She liked to buy ranch-style houses with an extra bedroom in the basement because: *You never know, Someone might need it, God is good.*

I would remember this later.

Rush and I had unpacked our first home in less than twenty-four hours. We took the biggest bedroom for ourselves, then I took another for my office. Room by room, I cordoned off the capriciousness of childhood. Here, pens would live in a brass cup, pads of paper in the desk drawer. Here, boxes would be broken down. At twenty-six, I was relieved to finally have some sense of autonomy. Here, our walls were our own.

Until they weren't again.

It's hard to remember what happened between those walls during our first two years, perhaps because it was unremarkably wonderful. I studied. Rush painted. We purchased cable television. It is one of life's great injustices how easily wonderful verges on boring. But it did, somehow. After several years of settling in, our home had started to feel hollower. The hardwood floors whined. The laundry thrummed. Even the guest room had started to smell less like fresh plastic and more like an empty drawer.

So, when a kitchen renovation at their house went long, Kevin and Emma packed their bags for ours. We even bought a wooden bench for their suitcases to sit on.

I never expected to like having houseguests so much. Emma and I would sit on the back porch, fanning ourselves with feminist theology books. Kevin and I would watch *Jeopardy* together, slurping soup off of tray tables in my office. At the time, all three of us had the happy luxury of a graduate student's schedule. Often there was food being cooked and drinks being poured when Rush got home from work with little forethought or cleanup required. Two adults were starting to seem too few to manage a modern life.

Still, they had their home and we ours. The week before they moved out, Emma got it in her head to make a cast of her big, watermelon belly. Would Rush like to help? she wondered. Now, Rush *was* an art major in college but not *that* kind of art major. (That he is not the Bohemian I would like him to be is one of the great letdowns and reliefs of our marriage.) And so, he declined and suggested a mutual friend instead, who came over one weekday night to wrap Emma's naked body in plaster of paris.

Listening to their sniggers behind the guest room door, Rush and I sat facing one another, feet touching, on the leather couch in our living room. I squeezed his ankle. He responded to my touch with a wink. It was lovely to feel useful but not especially needed. We had provided a space, and others had seen fit to fill it.

Could one make a life out of this?

There was only one way of knowing.

I would have to give this way of life a title.

And so it came to be that sometime in my late twenties, after Kevin and Emma moved out and before the girls moved in, I pronounced myself, "Minister of Availability." My tagline? Making space for neighbors while they make space for babies.

A Haven from the World

That I needed to validate this way of life with a title could be seen as a sorry sort of pomp. Why, I wonder now, had it been so important to me to sound important? Or, more to the point, useful? What had I internalized about the uselessness of my childless existence that had me so eager to show its worth?

Since Janell's visit, a stack of uneven books has been building on my fireplace mantel. Books about mothering. Books about biology. Books about infertility. As far as I know, Rush and I are not infertile. There are times when I wish we had tested his sperm or my egg count so that we had a fact to offer all who asked. A fact seemed easier to explain than a feeling, or a failure of feeling. A woman with a failure of feeling for the duty of motherhood is, from what I'm reading, something of an American tragedy.

Even a brief survey of the history of motherhood in

America will turn up a speech given by President Theodore Roosevelt in 1905 in which he famously shamed women who bartered a life of motherhood's "joy and sorrow" for one of "cold selfishness."[2] To modern sensibilities, the characterization isn't all that surprising. A recent anthology sums up the criticism of those who opt out of parenting nicely: *selfish, shallow*, and *self-absorbed*. So, there's that to contend with.

But it's the strategy behind Roosevelt's rhetoric and its lasting effects that I find more insidious. His audience for the speech was the National Congress of Mothers, an organization that sought to celebrate motherhood as not *inevitable* but *vocational*; pioneers of the child welfare movement, they believed raising, educating, and advocating for the next generation of children required more than good instincts; it required skill and support. (The National Congress of Mothers would go on to become the National Parent Teacher Association, better known as your friendly PTA.) It was a promising premise. But as it sometimes goes, politics ate promising for breakfast.

You see, children could no longer remain a natural consequence of sex or even a cheap, if precarious, labor force if women were going to feel responsible for them. And someone needed to *feel* responsible for them, didn't they? The National Congress of Mothers had been researching the conditions of children in the United States since 1897.[3] Incarcerated minors were in prisons with adults. Orphans went unprotected.

Children worked in mines. Certainly, these were injustices to be redressed.

Emphasizing the protection of children, however, had the unfortunate side effect of emphasizing the service of mothers as "the first and greatest duty of womanhood." Roosevelt was effusive on this point, so effusive that he cast the woman's duty in the home as more important even than the man's duty in the field or factory, proclaiming, "No built-up wealth, no splendor of material growth, no brilliance of artistic development, will permanently avail any people unless its home life is healthy."[4]

This was a new idea, mind you.

PRIOR TO THE turn of the twentieth century in America, home was not exactly "where the heart is," as they say. Think more utilitarian than utopian. According to historian Stephanie Coontz, the word *family* in Western civilization originally referred to a group of slaves, and only later came to refer to people related by blood or contract.[5] Marriage legitimized the exchange of property—and sex. Children were a way to make nations—and livings. The household was a site of economic opportunity—and, often, oppression.

This is not to say that no meaning was derived from domestic relationships, only that the home was considered subject rather than superior to civic life. The United States was indeed founded upon the principle that private values like loyalty, love, and ambition needed the civilizing influence of a public sphere that prized the common good alongside individual interests. Women in the new nation played an important role in politics as "republican mothers" or mothers who advocated for the welfare of all Americans, not just those living under their own roof.

So, what happened?

A lot of things. The Enlightenment emphasized the separation of the rational from the emotional. The Industrial Revolution emphasized the separation of the individual from the collective. By the late-nineteenth century, a new division of labor had effectively separated economic life from domestic life and White, middle-class women's participation in it. As a result, the home went from being a place where duties were performed by men and women alike to a place where exclusively feminine duties, like child-rearing, were lauded as a civilizing counterweight to marketplace individualism. It was a sweeping reversal of moral influence.

Home became the cornerstone of virtue, and mothers its most celebrated masons.

In light of this historical overview, the wall art at my local craft store makes some sense. *Love begins at home. Family comes first. Bless this nest.* "Have you ever considered how odd the metaphor of a nest is for a human home?" a colleague asks me. "It's almost as if a home isn't really a home unless it's in the service of raising children." That's exactly right, I tell her. A home without children was, according to Roosevelt, just "some flat, designed to furnish with the least possible expenditure of effort, the maximum of comfort and of luxury."

BY THE TIME President Roosevelt addressed the National Congress of Mothers in the early twentieth century, a new economic system had effectively been built that thrived off a rhetoric of contrasts. For men to be competitive in the world, women now had to provide haven from it in the home.

This move toward what's been called the "spiritualization of the home" in America depended on two key assumptions: one, that women were morally superior to men, and two, that motherhood wasn't just the highest duty; it was also the highest blessing. This strikes me now as the most perverse and lasting legacy of President Roosevelt's speech, best summed up in its emotional climax:

> The woman's task is not easy—no task worth doing is easy—but in doing it, and when she has done it, there shall come to her the highest and holiest joy known to mankind; and having done it, she shall have the reward prophesied in Scripture; for her husband and her children, yes, and all people who realize that her work lies at the foundation of all national happiness and greatness, shall rise up and call her blessed.

I might have believed Roosevelt, too, if he hadn't been so adamant that those who didn't make motherhood their world were any less blessed. (Even those who desired only two children are chastised in the speech for having "forgotten the primary laws of their being," a sterling example of natural theology at play.) But his anxiety, I think, betrays a less benevolent aim. A country can deflect welfare responsibilities if it casts the home as a public service. A country can grow faster, cheaper if it casts reproduction as a woman's purpose.

Does this all sound too cynical? Capitalism has that effect on me. I share this only to explain, and perhaps mostly to myself, what I think the strategy was behind Roosevelt's *selfish* claim. To put it crudely, women are meant to feel for their own homes, their own children, precisely so that men—and the government—are free not to. *Selfish* then, I can console myself, has less to do with the character flaws of women who aren't making motherhood their duty and more to do with the character flaws of a nation that believes it needs the unpaid labor of homemakers to prosper. There is, mind you, the matter of all that "built-up wealth" and "material growth."

It was maternal exceptionalism at its finest to believe that a mother's sense of purpose could only be propped up if nonmoms were cut down. But what Roosevelt and so many others who have hurled the same *selfish* accusations in his wake seem to miss is that, for some of us, not making motherhood our duty is precisely why we're free to serve our country or community.

And why we sometime give ourselves a ridiculous title to prove it.

Neighbors, but Which Neighbors?

President Roosevelt had conflated national duty with Christian duty, as if the two were obviously and easily compatible. But as I understood it, home was not my highest duty; devotion was. To God, firstly, or the universal source. To myself, also, or my personal, "genuine" source. These root devotions, however, were meant to inspire and sustain the outcropping of a third devotion: to my neighbors. At twenty-eight and with a recently vacated house, the question was: Which neighbors?

Kevin and Emma welcomed a fine baby into the world. The moment we got word their boy had arrived, Rush and I initiated launch. What did new parents need? I didn't know. They were among the first I'd seen up close. Were you supposed to bring food? Was it too soon for a flask? Panicked, we set off for the hospital with a used comedy DVD and the blind belief that what new parents need most is a good laugh.

Two years earlier, when we had moved from the San Francisco Bay Area, children were still being weighed and often delayed. In Durham—a progressive enclave, no doubt, but one still rooted in the American South—the lower cost of living and higher emphasis on tradition meant a greater focus on the nuclear family. Many of our new friends had the means to both buy a house and begin their brood. It was adapt-or-die time for a childfree couple like Rush and me if we wanted to make a life in which friends were like family.

Now, honestly, until that point, our "availability" had never struck me as notable. I thought we were just two under-whelming under-schedulers, Rush easily content with a Viking novel and I easily overwhelmed by, well, the telephone. We were homebodies through and through with a craving for margin that, if anything, felt like a liability for regular human contact. But as new parents hunkered down and focused in on their first kids, I began to see our unsung idleness as a quickly maturing asset.

Without kids of my own, when friends had a bellyful of baby or breasts full of milk, I learned about feeding schedules and sleeping schedules and how there was less time between either than I ever imagined. Not able to come to us because Willow's napping? Fine, let us come to you. Not doing dairy because Scout has reflux? We'll thicken our broth with flour.

Without kids of my own, when friends needed an afternoon walk instead of an afternoon drink, I gathered my things and planned for three—me, her, and baby. Three of us ambling down the sidewalk. Three of us lazing at the park. Three of us looking in three different directions. Me at her. Her at baby. Baby at filthy, playground toy.

Without kids of my own, I made new friends as I watched and waited for the shape of my old friends' lives to shake out. A colleague recommended I spend time with people outside my age group for a while—a twenty-two-year-old here, a fifty-nine-year-old there. I widened my circle by widening my hobbies—a pop-up chorus here, a wine and design there. I graduated from divinity school. I published my first book.

Still, there was room.

Around that same time, I purchased a coupon for a month of hot yoga. The class was dark and smelly and comprised of too many people in European-cut swimsuits. But it was worth the price for the mantra our instructor would sing over us week in and week out: "Everything is normal. And everything is temporary."

SHE WAS RIGHT, of course.

The "ministry of availability" was turning out to be a bust. I'd imagined our lives would be radically reordered by our small acts of service. But little had changed. I was not changed. I wanted to be *somewhat* changed.

There were two things to blame, as I saw it. One, Southern Self-Sufficiency. And two, My Own Damn Smugness.

Southern Self-Sufficiency is like Midwest Nice, but sweeter, harder to read. There were plenty of "Thanks so much" and "Aren't y'all kind?" when we offered to babysit for friends, but they were often followed by "We wouldn't want you to catch our cold" or "The grandparents are in town again." There was little that made me madder than being rebuffed for grandparents. Grandparents poked cracks in all the promises we'd

made in our early twenties: to do it differently, to do it together.

Which brought me to the second piece of all those missed
connections: My Own Damn Smugness. I wondered if all
that spaciousness made me feel superior to the overwhelmed
new parents. I wondered if I made it hard to want my help.
One time, a friend shared an achy parenting moment with
me over text, and I wrote back quickly, What do you need?
When she admitted she didn't know what she needed, I texted
a glib, Well, let me know when you do.

I wish someone had told me then that in those moments
the best help is given, not offered. You drop off the box of Joe-
Joe's without asking about allergies. You sweep in for an hour
of kidsitting with a freak-out-friendly plan in place. You
e-mail out of the blue with an unequivocal You are a marvel,
lady. You do not wait for permission to lean into love. Even if
your friends with children are, sometimes, hard to love. You
are hard to love, too.

"Are you *sure* sure we don't want a baby?" I asked Rush
while driving home from visiting another friend with another
newborn who was fine. They were all fine. But the "ministry of
availability" had never been about them. It had been about her.
A childless friend once put it perfectly, "Do I want to hold my
friend's baby? Okay. But more than anything I want to hold my
friend holding her baby." I wondered, would having a baby of
my own make the distance between me and her feel smaller?

I wasn't *sure* sure I didn't want one. But I was pretty sure, sure enough that I'd made Rush agree to marry me on the condition that my mind could not be expected to change, even though life inevitably would. He responded as casually as ever, "I'm good without one," and gunned our compact car through the widening intersection.

It was hard to tell if we were racing from something or toward something.

THE ANSWER GREETED us when we pulled into our gravel driveway. Twin peaks like eyebrows on the roof of our house raised in anticipation. The lunette on our yellow door grinned its upside-down smile. Our shaggy, red-headed mutt, Amelia, popped her face up in the window of our living room and locked onto us without letting go, as if we were Odysseus home from twenty years of troubles. We looked at one another and rolled our eyes, like people who don't know they're happy.

It was our home. Quiet space. Empty space. Space to think. Space to overthink. Space to paint and decorate and *re*paint and *re*decorate. For the first time in our adult life, we'd gotten hooked on home improvement shows; the idea that we had the power to design our own future—clean, modern, and with a farmhouse sink, please—was a cunning one. I think we knew that then. I think we knew that left unchecked we would become monsters of curation. Why else would we have decided that the deepest change worth chasing was in the place we loved and guarded most?

So, our physical space hadn't grown since our first long-term houseguests, but our feeling of capacity had. How much larger could we grow? We put feelers out to see if any friends needed a place to stay. Nothing. I suggested we consider housing refugees, but Rush wasn't so sure. We contemplated doing the cohousing thing, but I had been in those houses; the mismatched furniture alone made my minimalism twitch. What about opening up a retreat center in, say, ten years?

Looking back, I suppose the way we felt about our home was the way some people felt about their children: We were keen to count it as our community service. In that respect, we weren't so very different from those nineteenth-century homemakers who believed that to love your home was to love the world. After all, couldn't one argue that your children are a kind of neighbor? Couldn't we argue that our self-sufficient friends were a kind of neighbor, too?

The risk with this thinking—Janell once pointed out to me—is that sometimes you spend so much time loving your own home, resourcing your own children, tending your own friendships, that you never really make it to loving the world. Your world shrinks to sheepskin rugs and Amazon deliveries. Your neighbors shrink to the people with whom you share drinks or a bathroom. Don't get me wrong, I love this sort of shrinkage, only it did not seem to be the good life I read about under my crushed velvet covers.

The scriptures had far too much to say about neighbors who defied class comforts, who defied *my* comforts.[*]

A Haven for the World

Pastor Lisa bought her house in the southeast section of Raleigh. It's a new build in an old neighborhood called College Park that cropped up as an enclave for the Black middle class after the Civil War. While College Park has felt the strain in recent years from systemic poverty and soaring development, Lisa was keen to be grafted into its roots. To eat Popsicles on the front porch with her neighbors. To wait at bus stops in the morning with her neighbors' children. To practice a different way to make a home, including with herself, she says, "Because I am a family of one."

Tonight, I've been invited to Pastor Lisa's home for a

---

[*] Deuteronomy 15:7: "If there is among you anyone in need, a member of your community in any of your towns within the land that the Lord your God is giving you, do not be hard-hearted or tight-fisted toward your needy neighbor." / Proverbs 3:28–29: "Do not say to your neighbor, 'Go, and come again, tomorrow I will give it'—when you have it with you. Do not plan harm against your neighbor who lives trustingly beside you." / Luke 10:25–29: "A lawyer stood up to test Jesus. 'Teacher,' he said, 'what must I do to inherit eternal life?' He said to him, 'What is written in the law? What do you read there?' He answered, 'You shall love the Lord your God with all your heart, and with all your soul, and with all your strength, and with all your mind; and your neighbor as yourself.' And he said to him, 'You have given the right answer; do this, and you will live.' But wanting to justify himself, he asked Jesus, 'And who is my neighbor?'" / Gulp.

conversation about race and gender. To be clear, I don't usually call her Pastor with a capital P, but Lisa does lead the
young, multiracial church where I belong. Our list of values is
short. To name a few: "We show up." "Our language is blessing." "Race is always on the table." This last one means we
commit to regularly asking the question, How is race at play
here? Here in our church, our neighborhood. Here inside ourselves, in the invisible crevices, where we've been shaped to
believe who and what is worth feeling for.

A small group of us sit around the perimeter of Lisa's living
room now, carefully eating Mediterranean food on her white
sectional and answering the questions of a friendly researcher,
here in town studying Black clergywomen and their congre-
gations. As theology talk ebbs and flows throughout the night,
I try hard not to be a nerd. I have to repeatedly shove tabouli
in my mouth to keep from speaking out of turn.

But as it often goes, the real magic happens after the official part is over, and Lisa and I are left cleaning up in the
kitchen. She and I are moving swiftly, consolidating pita into
plastic containers, when the conversation turns to how it's
tough enough being a Black clergywoman, let alone a childless one. I stop, lean hard against the cool, stone island, and
listen.

"Black women are expected to be mothers," Lisa starts, adding, "and surrogate mothers! We're expected to be mothers to
other people's children, and then somehow have time leftover
to tend our own." She shakes her head. "I mean, you wouldn't

believe how surprised people are to find I've gotten this far in life without a child coming through my"—she makes a dramatic downward V motion with both hands—"underground railroad."

I laugh without meaning to.

The stereotype, I later learn, comes from antebellum America where African slave women were cast as Mammies and Jezebels. Natural caregivers to White children. Willing sexual partners to White men. Social surrogates for White women. Their bodies put in service of building other people's homes. You might even say that Black women were meant to feel for White people's homes precisely so that White people—and the government—were free not to.

"It's funny, you know," I pause, a little embarrassed over my new research obsession. It does not stop me from citing statistics in casual conversation. "There's a perception that childlessness is a phenomenon particular to Whiteness. But it's not. Not for American-born women. The percentages aren't dramatically different across different races."[6]

"No, childless just has different stigmas for women of color," Lisa explains, rubbing a towel along the edge of a tumbler.

I've read about this, too. How some people consider it not only *unnatural* for a Black or Brown woman to be childless but also *unfaithful*, a disgrace to their race. In one magazine article, an American woman of Mexican Honduran descent described how the continuation of future generations is the mark of hard-won success in her immigrant family—to break that cycle is a tragedy akin to treason.[7] In another article, a Black woman shared how after telling a brother she didn't intend to have children, he shot back, "That's just what the white man wants," as if it mattered little what she wanted.[8]

So for oppressed groups, reproduction may not be a national duty—both President Roosevelt and the National Congress of Mothers have been tied to the eugenicist belief that only the "racially fit" (epitomized by Anglo-Saxon Americans) had a responsibility to breed—but reproduction may be construed as an ethnic duty; having children is one way of not being erased, one way of saying we survived, even this, even still.[9]

"So, do *you* ever worry about being called selfish or, I don't know, unfaithful?" I ask Lisa, my voice pitchy, unsure. I pretend to brush some crumbs into my hand as cover.

Lisa sighs, stepping away from the now cleared-out sink. "I remember being afraid when I was younger that people would judge me for not having the thing that other people talk about. For not having maternal instincts, for being less of a woman. That I must not love or know how to care for children. That I wouldn't be able to speak into their lives."

I let out a low whistle.

"But, no, I no longer feel like I'm selfish," she says, a smile rising through her cheekbones. "My very vocation binds me to children and families. I'm actually making a strong statement that they don't have to belong to me in a particular way but I'm saying yes to them. And I love that. I love that the church gets you into situations you never signed up for."

But that Christians *have* made a particular kind of relationship to children and family into evidence of a divine blessing or duty well done is a real problem for those Lisa pastors. She hears stories of singles who wonder how many more prayer journals they're going to have to write before being worthy of marriage. Or stories of women who can't get pregnant or don't want to get pregnant and fear their life will be judged as lacking. "It's doing something really dangerous to people that they can't just sit and be and feel like they're enough," she says.

She wipes her hands on a dishrag and leans back to survey her house, now nearly clean from the evening's gathering. The silence hangs between us like a satisfying yawn. "You know, I wake up in the morning and I actually have enough energy to stand at the bus stop with the children who live in my neighborhood. And maybe it's because I'm not sleep-deprived or because I'm not trying to nurse a child. One is not better or worse than the other. It's just that this is my life. And I don't want to add semicolons, or caveats. No, I showed up."

I think to myself that Lisa is right. It doesn't matter how you get there but that you get there. Show up to your own life. Move into the neighborhood. Make your home, children or no children, in such a way that you have room left to love the tender world beyond it. Open your desire like a door and ask how it might, impossibly as the poet Alice Walker says, transform into something like devotion.

Driving home that night, I let my memories remake me. Surely, if I had followed my desire alone, I would not have become a mother at all, not a biological one, not an adoptive one, not even a spiritual one. I am too much of a misanthrope for that. But now that I think about it, it wasn't solely a selfless call to duty, either, that drew us to consider a purpose as farfetched as fostering. It was both. Our desire to make a home, slowly, grew into a devotion to our neighbors, and our devotion to our neighbors, slowly, grew into a desire to house our neighbors' children.

The Next Best Step

I still remember the conversation at the borrowed beach house. It rained all the way through our first full day there. On the second, it was barely two o'clock by the time Rush and I began day-drinking. Condensation crept down our wineglasses, the shuttered windows, our elbow pits. Bored, I propped my back against the slip-covered couch and pulled up a training schedule for prospective foster parents on my laptop.

On a whim, I had attended a fostering recruitment meeting the month before. A group of well-mannered White people sat around drinking coffee out of foam cups. Everything about it was stale except the stories. Stories of bodies being

given and taken away, of marriages being stretched and ne-
glected, of families being torn and mended. A gray-haired
woman said the training alone was worth the trouble for the
kind of friends-like-family that formed in it. She said people
brought fried chicken to class.

"This is ridiculous," I said to Rush, snapping my laptop
closed, the skin on my thighs red from the heat. "We couldn't
even make one of these trainings if we wanted to with our
work schedules."

For all our talk of availability, it was apparently hard to be
predictably available, inconveniently available to one thing.

"Well, I guess that settles it." I yawned. "I'm not willing to
rearrange my calendar for this, are you?"

Rush looked up from the high-top table where he sat play-
ing solitaire. "No, not really."

He shrugged.

I shrugged.

We broke the moment with a laugh.

"We're the worst," I said and chugged the last swish
of wine.

I cannot say with certainty what compelled us to return to
the idea of fostering, again and again. But it wasn't "for the
children," as they say. (It would be months before we realized
children were indeed ninety percent of the endeavor.) It was
for the promise of community, uncurated and uncharted community, both with others in the foster training, yes, but also
with social workers and birth parents and court clerks. You

know, the kind of community one can usually only find at the DMV. We had begun to romanticize this unlikely community in the same way thirtysomething friends had begun talking about land, more land, as the answer to the questions still forming in our restless hearts.

Three weeks after our beach trip, I discovered a foster parenting session beginning in January that Rush and I could both attend. There was never any long, drawn-out discussion about whether we'd do it. We just took the next step, then the next best one after that. We put the "orientation informational session" for the class on the calendar. We agreed not to plan any more travel. Other than that, nothing. No reading. No researching. No planning.

I joked to a friend that it was like we were engaged in the nonbiological equivalent of "taking the goalie out." Not actively trying to conceive a new life yet. Just curious about whether one was possible.

CHAPTER 3

Script: Motherhood Is the Toughest Job

Rewrite: Motherhood, Like a Lot of Work, Is a Profession of Faith

The world has our hands, but our soul belongs to Someone Else.
—ABRAHAM JOSHUA HESCHEL[1]

BY THE MORNING of the "orientation informational session," Rush and I were properly panicked.

What had we been thinking? Not planning? Not researching? Not reading that the "orientation informational session" required advance registration?

Still in my pajamas, body bent over the hulking, weathered-oak desk in my office, I cringed while he stood behind me and read aloud from the website: "'This session is by invitation only. To register, please contact the Inquiry Line.'"

"I know," I said without him saying.

"But I thought it was only an information session."

"An *orientation informational session*," I repeated.

"Well, what the hell does that mean? Is it orientational or informational?"

I turned to face him with a stiff grin.

"Welcome to government communication."

Rush collapsed onto my nap couch, moss green in color with drool stains as big as lily pads. He cupped his hands over his eyes. I didn't console him.

Then, after a few mournful breaths of silence, "Where's your phone?" I asked.

"Why?" He moaned.

"*'To register, please contact the Inquiry Line.'*"

Harriet answered on the first ring. Her voice was professional, old-fashioned, like a woman who used hot rollers and neck moisturizer. When I told her my husband and I were interested in registering for tonight's "orientation informational session," she responded with what sounded like mock sweetness, "I'm sorry, ma'am. I already have a waitlist for that session. People have been registered since September." It was December now. She continued in her quest to appear helpful, "But I can take down your information for when you come to the next one."

My throat closed. The six-week training, starting in January, was the only one listed in the coming year that was compatible with our current jobs. We needed this December prerequisite if we wanted to get on with deciding what to do with our very important lives. And we did. We hoped to cross off potential life paths as swiftly and efficiently as if they were grocery items on our chalkboard wall: *eggs, almond milk, fos-*

tering. The chalk, its stroke of simple accomplishment, felt good in our hands.

Our jobs at the time, I should clarify, were not overly demanding or burdensome. We were not in the military. We were not healthcare or oil rig workers. We were not even what you'd call workhorses. Rush held a forty-hour-a-week position at a local church where he dazzled coworkers with his ability to use a Google calendar. I, on the other hand, had the fortune of a part-time facilitation contract that paid the equivalent of a full-time salary, leaving hours enough to write and walk and even nap most days.

The difficulty was our days rarely looked the same. We both traveled consistently, cheerfully, for event-based work.

So, we were not married to our jobs, but we were in a committed relationship with our jobs, a commitment I was not yet sure was compatible with the commitment of parenting. How then was I supposed to tell Harriet, who was breathing softly on the other end of the line, that I wasn't sure about giving her our time, let alone giving her our names?

But, because pauses make me panic, I said, "Sure," and, reluctantly, gave in to the impromptu interview.

So, I told her our names.

And then I told her what we took home in pay every month but failed to say mine was variable. Children in foster care didn't need more variables, from what I'd gathered.

When she asked what Rush did for a living, I said, "Youth

pastor." When she asked me what I did for a living, I said, "Retreat facilitator," because it sounded more plausible than "Writer."

I told her that we had a three-bedroom house, but only one was available for children; the other was my office, my closed door, my ode to not giving up on myself. The weathered-oak desk had been a gift from Rush on my thirtieth birthday, a symbol of his confidence in my work, should my own ever waver.

I told her that we wanted to foster because we "felt gifted in hospitality" and "wanted to share our home with others."

These answers felt both agreeable and true.

At the end of her line of questioning, Harriet delicately cleared her throat and said, "Well, I like that your husband is a youth pastor. You can come to tonight's session."

"What?" I sputtered, immediately putting her on speakerphone. Rush shot up from the spongey couch, his arms raised above his head in dumb shock.

"There may not be room for you in the January training, but at least you'll know what you're in for."

"Yes. Thank you. We really appreciate it," I said, my voice reaching into a new register.

She added, with a well-rehearsed lilt of indifference, "I can't promise anything."

"I know."

Neither could I.

A Profession of Overwhelm

There were plenty of good reasons for me to be cautious about the cost of modern parenting.

If in the late nineteenth century American motherhood had been pitched as national duty, in the twentieth century it was rebranded as personal profession. The push for child welfare protections had worked. Which meant children no longer went to work. Which meant children *became* work.

While once the household economy had been a family affair, after World War II, the focus shifted from children laboring for their parents to parents laboring for their children.[2] And there was no one who clocked in more childcare hours than a mother. Motherhood was fast on its way to becoming "the toughest job in the world."

But if motherhood is a job, then I decide it's an insulting one.

This much is clearer to me after watching a recent advertisement from card company American Greetings. I go online to search for the video after reading about it in one of the growing number of books that has crept from my fireplace mantel to the corner of my desk. It's as awful as I hoped.

The setup goes like this: American Greetings posted a fake job opening and then recorded real interviews with both men and women applicants. The title? Director of

Operations. The requirements? Standing up most or all of the time without breaks; degrees in medicine, finance, and the culinary arts; no vacations—with an increase in workload over the holidays. And, the interviewer adds, "If you had a life, we'd sort of ask you to give that life up." Oh, and the job is 365 days a year without pay. The punch line? There are already billions of people who hold this position: moms.

You can guess people's initial reactions to what the interviewer calls "Not just any job but probably the most important one." Intense. Inhumane. One woman asks of the "no breaks" rule, "Is that even legal?" But once the punch line is revealed and the inspirational music rolls out, the unrealistic expectations for motherhood are met not with outrage but gratitude. The interviewees are baited into gratitude for their own moms. "They meet every requirement, don't they?" The interviewer laughs without irony. And so did millions of others as the #worldstoughestjob video went viral.

Forgive me for saying so, but that is some sadistic shit.

So, why do I enjoy watching it? What is it about women being recognized as the equivalent of unpaid interns who will do anything *for the experience* that is infuriating but also validating? Why is other people's pain validating? Do moms have to be validated as the tough*est* to be worthy? Doesn't this superlative spew ignorance at other kinds of caregiving? And is any of this a helpful way to feel more human? It doesn't help me; after a brief spike of glee, I just feel lonely. Lonely because parenting *is* hard. Lonely because I don't want another job, and further, I already require an obscene number of breaks to get through a day, breaks so numerous as to be deemed insubordinate.

It's hard not to miss that consumerism is at the heart of American rhetoric about motherhood. The American Greetings advertisement, after all, is meant to entice adult children to purchase a store-bought card on Mother's Day, a holiday that was later denounced by its childless founder for excessive commercialization. (You can't make this up.)

Anna Jarvis established the commemorative day in 1908 as a way to honor her deceased mother's work on behalf of women and children and to counterbalance society's undue focus on men's achievements. She hoped the day would serve as a reminder to write or visit one's own mother, even attend one's "mother" church.

But by the time it became a national holiday in 1914, "Mother's Day" had been turned into merchandise. Jarvis eventually became so jaded by the unofficial proliferation of carnations, confections, and branded menu items (it's reported that she once ordered a "Mother's Day Salad" at the Wanamaker Department Store only to dramatically toss it on the floor), that by the time she died in 1948, she had spent nearly all her fortune and free time lobbying to cut it from our calendars.[3]

So, the veneration of motherhood sells. Only now, plenty of women are no longer sold on its exchange rate.

TAKE MY FRIEND Margaret. Children were not her true love. Nor was the man she married at twenty-three. But the man wanted children, and she was open to it. However, after years of trying and failing, eventually the marriage failed, too. She was divorced by twenty-nine.

While Margaret says being childless—although she wouldn't call it that—wasn't a conscious choice, she's come to embrace a life without biological children. (When asked the inevitable *Do you have kids?* question, she usually describes the relationship she enjoys with her niece and nephews, undermining another consumer assumption that "to have" kids is "to own" them exclusively.) She's realized that modern motherhood requires a level of commitment, stamina, and brain drain that she doesn't have or want to give.

Over video chat one Saturday morning, while I'm indulging in the quiet of work and Rush is taxiing the girls to a volleyball tournament, she tells me, "So often you see people with families, and they're really overwhelmed."

Fair enough.

Overwhelm is the smog a lot of parents breathe these days. Brigid Schulte, author of the book *Overwhelmed: Work, Love, and Play When No One Has the Time*, cites a number of contributing factors, most centered on work and family in the

United States.[4] To start, Americans work among the most hours in the world, with white-collar workers putting in longer hours and blue-collar workers cobbling together more jobs than ever before. That same relentless work ethic carries over to the home, where working mothers now spend, on average, more time attending to their children (11 hours a week) than *all* mothers did in the sixties.[5,6] Fathers spend more time on childcare, too, tripling their average from 2.5 hours a week in 1965 to about 8 hours a week some fifty years later.[7]

The work and family balance has become so elusive that Stewart D. Friedman, founding director of the Wharton Work/ Life Integration Project, points to it as one of the primary causes behind the rising number of childless Millennials. In a cross-generational study of University of Pennsylvania men and women undergrads, Friedman asked the Gen X class of 1992 and the Millennial class of 2012, "Do you plan to have or adopt children?" Seventy-nine percent of Gen X women interviewed answered, "Yes," compared to only 43 percent of Millennial women interviewed twenty years later. The numbers were nearly identical for the men. Notably, the amount of hours respondents expected to work had grown from 58 hours per week to a whopping 72. Friedman sees the two statistics as related.[8]

So, if the "toughest job in the world" pitch is meant to be a recruitment tool, it's a terrible one. This comes up in a number of my conversations with childless women who tell me that they have few to no examples of mothers leading lives worth imitating. Iris says, "There is not one single person who has a child that I'm like, 'Oh my God, I want that life.' Not one!" Melody, a writer and professor, observes, "My female friends have married great men, and yet they still do eighty percent of the childcare . . . I absolutely believe motherhood specifically, not fatherhood or parenthood, is the hardest job to do well. It's just not one I could do well. I wouldn't want to."

IT IS, I think, a missed point of connection that some of the people who respect a parent's job the most are the ones who have opted out of it entirely. Indeed, it's because Margaret takes seriously the work of mothers that she no longer thinks it's the right work for her. Margaret resonates with Oprah on this, who famously chose not to have children, "because something [in my life] would have had to suffer and it would've probably been them."[9]

Margaret has been criticized for this kind of reasoning. People have told her it's small-minded to think she can't be a parent and professional. Or made the assumption that now she's destined to be a "career woman" whose life is dedicated to work alone. One friend, a mother of four, was so upset, thinking that Margaret wasn't taking the decision seriously enough, that she refused to speak to her for a whole year.

I'd like to believe there are plenty of modern mothers who are figuring out how to follow their occupational thread without ripping apart at the seams. (I would like to believe I am one of them.) It often takes some serious boundary-setting, caregiving that can be counted on, and a philosophy that good is "good enough." Piles of money help. It also, however, takes a diffuse focus that may not feel as sure or satisfying or beneficial as a more singular one.

Interestingly, through the Wharton Work/Life Integration Project, Freidman found that the more a woman wanted to be engaged in providing social value through her work, the less likely it was that she would become a mother. Friedman reflects, "It's almost as if there's a competition between serving the family of humanity versus the family that you might create with your own children." He adds, "It's just not true."[10]

Perhaps not. We need to do better by mothers and parents more broadly in this country. I think most of us can agree on that. But we also need to do better by women discerning whether they want to be mothers at all. We need to tell them about the trade-offs of being a modern parent. And we can't fault them for looking at the fault lines of the great work and family debate and saying, "No, thank you."

Margaret believes that when we "say no to say yes" we can create breathing space in our lives that benefits our whole community. At thirty-eight years old, she's created breathing space to accomplish some astonishing things, like writing a book on embracing one's natural hair, earning a PhD in leadership studies, and mentoring people who want to reframe love as an ethic rather than an achievement.

"It doesn't matter whether you're married, single, divorced, childfree, have children—society's going to always tell you you should be doing something else. You're not doing enough. You're doing too much," Margaret tells me. "But I say think about the time you do have, wherever you are, and use that time to invite joy into your life in ways you might not have expected because you were looking for it somewhere else."

It occurs to me while talking to her, aware that my own hushed morning is fast becoming as slippery as sand, that the marketplace wants to sell us on our own scarcity. But instead of worrying about what we're missing out on, Margaret says, we'd be better off wondering about what we're being invited into.

We Need All Kinds of Kinds

Which leads me back to how we began fostering some four years ago. Parenting did not look easy—charming, at times, but not easy—and if our white-collar friends did not need our help, then surely someone did. Surely, we needed all kinds of people, with all kinds of jobs, to play all kinds of parts in our community. Surely, someone could work with our kind.

The "orientation informational session" took place downtown, in a modern building across the street from cellblock housing. I tried to let Rush walk ahead of me; he's always two steps behind, and I hate to be the first to enter a room. But every time I slowed down, he slowed down behind me. When we got to the second floor, room A, he opened the door and gestured for me to enter.

"You first," I pushed.

The room was clean, brightly lit. It smelled like dry-erase markers. Folding tables made a three-sided square around the perimeter, with a projector in the middle. We signed in and sat down, a meticulously organized folder placed at each of our seats. It was at this moment I decided I could get used to working with the government, what with our shared love of paperwork.

The hour began with a video, an adequate video as far as videos go, about a teenager who was put into foster care. In one scene, the foster mother gives the teen a dress that reminds her of her birth mother. Teen unfolds in a fit. Teen slams the door. Foster mother cries. I tried to suppress an eye roll, looking around the room for validation. That kind of behavior was to be expected, right? We weren't supposed to take it personally, right? A classmate two tables over put her hand to her heart and mouthed a frowny "oh" to her partner.

Next, we moved to a presentation on the prerequisites for foster parents. There were big things: like passing a background check. And there were small things: like no interior lock-and-key in your house. At this, a single woman shot her hand up into the air and asked, "Is the lock a deal breaker? Because not having an interior lock is a total security risk." Yes, deal breaker. At this, she threw up her hands. "Well, I'm out then."

It happened again and again. Scanning the sterile conference room, I noticed other prospective parents' eyes narrow when mine widened, mouths droop when mine twitched, breath inhale when mine exhaled. There was something uncanny about the way fostering seemed to fit my misfit tendencies. All the things that should have turned me off— the promise of rejection, the random rules—didn't, by some strange logic. And all the things that felt like deficits in me— my ambivalence about newborns, my appetite for deep and uninterrupted sleep—weren't, actually, when the stated goal was to love and let go and the need was for parents of older, wake-up-later kids. Here, my limits gleamed like precious jewels under the fluorescent light.

The session ended unceremoniously with questions and answers, but my ballooning thoughts were too big for the time allotted. They began taking flight on the car ride home with Rush. "Do we even have the capacity for this?" "And what if we don't enjoy it, because I want to really *enjoy* it?" "And, also, what are we going to do about that nude painting of me in the guest bedroom?"

I stopped talking, too out of breath to realize the question of *if* we were going to foster was slipping into *how* we were going to foster.

Rush took his hand off the wheel and squeezed my shoulder. I gave his knuckles a hard flick, not in the mood to be soothed.

"Listen." He laughed. "We may not have much freedom in

how we prepare our home or who we parent with. But at least we have the freedom to say no if it's not working. That's more than most parents get, right?"

The thought calmed me. *No* had always been a steady friend. *No* had good manners, clear boundaries. *No* left parties at 9 p.m. *Yes* came into your house and ate all the good cereal, leaving the bowl in the sink without rinsing.

"So, what are you saying? Are we going to do the January class?" I pressed.

"I think we can't not do it," he said.

And I knew what he meant.

A Profession of Faith

Retelling the story now, one question is embarrassingly obvious to me: Wasn't fostering my own little attempt at having it all, too? In truth, hadn't I been even more ambitious than most? To believe it possible to maintain a commitment not only to the fabled foes of career and children, but also to nonattachment, government oversight, and, for heaven's sake, sleeping in? By what logic did I think this feat of equanimity possible?

And yet to some extent is *has* been possible.

I start a list, this one not in chalk but ink, of all that Rush and I had going in our favor when we set out, moving my thumb over each item like a rosary bead, offering penance for our advantages. We had a reasonable mortgage, for one, a generous down payment made possible by my parents' savings. And, further, we both had ridiculously flexible, rewarding jobs. Didn't those two things make nearly everything else easier?

Sure, we never jointly made more than ninety thousand dollars in a given year, and a hospital birth would have cost me a third of that without maternity insurance, but hadn't we always had enough for fresh produce and yearly tennis shoes and the occasional weekend away? Didn't it count for something that we were largely free to set our own schedules, to work from home, to labor over the hulking, weathered-oak desk, and to day-drool on the moss-colored couch?

This is a list that's keeping me honest, less dismissive, more understanding that parenting has always been tougher for some than for others. This is especially true for working mothers who have somehow in the last fifty years increased their participation in the workforce and family at the very same time. Having it all, whatever that tired phrase means, has never looked so hard, particularly in a country where scandalous workplace policies have mixed with a culture of intensive mothering.

Intensive mothering has been described as a "child-centered, expert-guided, emotionally absorbing, labor-intensive, and financially expensive" approach to raising children. (The description alone makes your eye twitch.) Aspects of this belief system have recently been found "detrimental to women's mental health"; like the belief that "women are the essential parent" or the belief that "parenting is challenging."[11] Yes, even *admitting* parenting is tough is proving royally obvious and unhelpful.

Which is probably why there's little that irritates me more than someone, other than my therapist, pointing this out now that I am parenting. Because I know. And I knew. And knowing that I knew—although how can any of us know before we know?—makes me feel basic and foolish and helpless. And that's it, isn't it? I would have preferred to stay the one giving the help than the one needing the help.

I wonder if this feeling of helplessness points to what exactly we find so tough about parenting. It is humiliating, in the truest sense of the word, meaning it reminds you and me that we are *humus*, from dust we come, to dust we shall return. Egos are leveled. Selves are emptied. The illusion that I can ever take a day "off" from being responsible for another human being is ruined.

But, and I feel very prickly about this, I am not ready to admit that parenting is especially humiliating, only reliably humiliating. Humiliation is an equal opportunity teacher.

So, HERE IS the best I can conclude. Motherhood may not be a job, but it is, like a lot of things we do, a *profession*. In the ancient world, a profession was not a paid occupation but a statement of faith. Parents profess faith in all kinds of things with our actions. Choosing to have a biological baby is faith that the planet can sustain another human life. Sending a child to public school is faith that what's accessible to most is what's best for mine. Letting Youngest watch her twelfth "funniest puppies" video in a row is faith that her brain won't rot while mine takes a break. But for the faithful there can be only one answer to where we bank our trust at the end of the day, and we're going to turn up empty if it's in something we do and not something divine. "The world has our hands," wrote Rabbi Abraham Joshua Heschel, "but our soul belongs to Someone Else."[12]

In other words, we can do hard things, but we are not defined by the hard things we do.

This must be one reason why my own mother, much to my amazement, describes parenting as easy. She likes being around people, which I do think helps immensely; the people part of parenting is a real bummer for me. But more importantly, she says she gave Charlie and me, her people, "back to God."

"What does that mean exactly?" I ask her one evening, while reheating dinner in the microwave. "Because I feel like I've tried giving my kids back to God but God keeps giving me their laundry."

So, she tells me how one day she was driving around town when a popular preacher came on the radio and started talking about how our children don't really belong to us. They belong to God. She sat in her car thinking this over. She had never heard of this idea before but, as a single mother, it freed something inside of her to know she wasn't parenting alone.

Hearing her tell the story over stale pizza, I imagine it must have freed her to know that our worth, her worth, wasn't up to her. It was already settled. It couldn't be muscled.

And so, I start a new list, not of the things Rush and I had going in our favor when we set out to foster, but the things we put our faith in. We had faith that we could have multiple callings, seasonal callings, and that the call to parenting didn't trump the call to ministry or the call to writing.

Another thing: We had faith that whatever external work parenting required—the appointments, the tournaments, the tutoring—the inner workings of a child's soul were out of our control; they happened by grace, in community, and with a disconcerting amount of mystery.

We also had faith that the same underwhelming, under-scheduling we had mastered in our childfree life could be a replicable skill in our parenting life. So, we agreed to limit, as much as humanly possible, the appointments, the taxiing, and the tutoring.

"Oh, but it's easier for you," a friend declared. "Anything you do for your children is gravy, given their backgrounds." But I did not see it this way.

To save space for the unexpected, we were learning, was

not just good hospitality to our neighbor but hospitality to the holy.

IT IS A hallmark of the middle class to put our worth into our work. Work is not just a commodity but an identity. I'm guilty of it, too. I don't just write; I'm a writer. I don't just lead retreats; I'm a facilitator. So it makes sense that the majority of American moms *do* think the work of mothering defines them. Whether this is because society socializes women to prize relationships above all else or because women do prize relationships above all else is hard to say. But, in recent years, fathers have begun to follow suit. The gap between mothers and fathers who say "parenting is extremely important to their identity" is now a single percentage point at 58 percent and 57 percent, respectively.[13] It's no wonder the investment of hours in a child's life could grow extremely competitive and intense.

I think back to the National Congress of Mothers and those would-be PTA ladies. For all the good that treating motherhood, and parenting more broadly, as a vocation has done—the increased protections for children, the deepened appreciation for domestic labor, the growing recognition that parents desperately need help—there's a dark side to it, too. When we make a relationship into an occupation, we're apt to treat it like one. More effort needed. More specialization required. More pressure piled on.

Our boneheaded American assumption is that tougher is better. We've made "doing hard things" into a matter of individual identity rather than a fact of collective life. Years earlier, when Rush and I were still childfree, I sometimes used a war metaphor (poor form, I know) to describe our calling to come alongside weary parents. If parents were among the front lines of life's heavy, then we were the respite workers who'd wipe their sweaty brows and bloodied knees when they came in from the fray. It made little sense to wonder which of us had chosen the more important part when, in the end, our fate was bound together.

Our Happy Terror

September 18, 2015

Dear Friends,

After completing a six-week course, along with a series of home visits, reference interviews, fire inspections, and good-natured body frisks, Rush and I are officially licensed foster parents. I've taken to describing what lies ahead as "our happy terror," and it is thrilling. It is thrilling like a trapeze artist who has jumped off the ledge and awaits that moment of connection. We are all limbs and possibilities. Consensual possibilities.

We responded to the first call about a potential foster placement with "Too soon! Call again in a month!" Another, and then another, came in, each time sending us into a panicked search for "The Binder" where I've typed a series of questions to ask the social workers. *Still in diapers? We're not comfortable procuring any additional, um, equipment. Only one of them? That seems like it would require a lot of sustained eye contact.* After each call, I look down and frown at the scribbles that mock all certainty.

Here is what we are certain of: We want to foster. We want to foster badly, so badly that we're willing to put all our eggs (and my egg-making years) in this basket.

As preparation for the transition, I've been meeting with a vocational coach so that I can remember who I am in this moment before letting go. When I told her I wanted to someday go off the grid, run a hostel, and practice hospitality to travelers coming through, she said it didn't sound all that different from fostering. Working for the government isn't exactly going off the grid, but it does mean considerably less e-mail, more drop-ins. I'm eager for it.

Our preparation has been a quiet one filled with travel-size toiletries laid out in twos, board games stacked high in the empty closet, and a twin bed lofted over our guest one. We're hoping for a sibling pair between the ages of 6–16. We're hoping that just like we're better together, they might be, too.

So be it,

Erin

Fashioning a Life Well-Lived

CHAPTER 4

Script: But You'd Make
a Great Mom

*Rewrite: Mother Makes a Better
Verb Than Noun*

*Even if we are not mothers, the noun, we may be mothering,
the verb. Indeed, unless mothering is a verb, it is a fact but not
a truth, a state but not an action.*
                                        —GLORIA STEINEM[1]

ONE YEAR AFTER beginning my informal interviews
with friends, I am off to attend a ten-day writing camp in Min-
nesota. The same week, Rush and the girls are scheduled to
attend a family reunion on the North Carolina coast. *Happy
coincidence*, I had written on my registration. His family is
lovely, really, but the sun and sand and shared bathrooms
make it hard to enjoy them properly. I don't imagine they enjoy me much either when I spend half the day hiding in a dark
bedroom with a book. However, if I am not the woman they
hoped for Rush, they do not say, and I love them more for it.

Now that I have traced my desire with Janell, now that I
have remembered my devotion with Lisa, now that I have re-
oriented my faith with Margaret, I have decided to try to

write about it. The "it" part is still unclear. Some people back home have heard that I am working on a book about being childfree. "Surely, you don't think you're still childfree?" they ask with puzzled looks. "What do your children think about your work?" others whisper. They are confused. And I can't blame them. I prepare fifty pages of a manuscript that I have no interest in finishing to share with my fellow campers.

Nevertheless, writing camp turns out to be heaven—or close to it. A Benedictine monastery sits across the lake from our compound of mid-century brick cottages where we eat, think, work, pray. A few black-robed monks grace the seminar room to pray for our writing. I think I would have made a good monk. Here I am largely alone with my thoughts. Here I yield to a rhythm I did not create. Here there are pickles in the lunch line and for some reason that feels like a luxury as sweet as a two-bedroom cottage all to myself.

I go out of my way to thank the woman responsible for the pickles, our camp program manager, whose gray hair shimmers like wet stone.

"The pickles make me feel like I have a mom again," I confess to her while a small group of us sits outside, swatting flies and shoveling food. "Not that you're my mom."

Forks hang in mid-air.

"Or that my mom is dead. She's not."

Mouths gape open.

"It's just that I don't buy pickles back home, too pricey."

She nods, before someone blessedly changes the subject.

For all my ambiguity around being a mom, I sure am keen to be mothered.

A Question for My Therapist, Part I

"So, am I the 'mom' now simply because I have a vagina?" It was a serious question for my therapist. Rush and I were a few months into our first (and last) foster placement when I noticed the word had begun trailing me like a shadow that was not my shape. Too tall, too narrow. Unsettling, really.

No one had prepared me for this eclipse, whereby women go from being a particular person to a generic person, from a name to a role. I'd read about it in anthropology books, how women around the world sometimes lost their names the more socialized they became. I just hadn't realized how common it was here in America, land of infinite progress.

To be fair, I knew women who didn't mind being referred to by their relational roles, even relished the arrival in their life of titles like *Wife* or *Mom*. But for the most part, they did seem partial to only their partner or child using them. Because it would be weird, yes, if your husband's boss turned to you at the company picnic and mused, "Now, what does Wife have to say about that?"

As for me, I was still very much attached to my first name. This worked out well given that the girls were still very much attached to their first mom. There had to be more women, I reasoned, who didn't fit the conventional shape of momness.

Moms who didn't feel like stereotypical moms. Non-moms doing the work of traditional moms. Foster moms and step-moms and grandma moms, who were not so easily defined.

Whatever the reasons, there are plenty of reasons to tread lightly in our assumptions. Yet, wherever I went—schools, dentist offices, dinner parties—the idea persisted that an adult woman accompanying a child was its mother—and further went by the title *Mom*, wanted to be called *Mom*, identified with the essence of *Mom* and all the exhausting expectations that came with it.

I HAD BEEN thinking about these expectations a lot since the girls' arrival.

It was December, a full year after the foster parent orientation, when we received the initial call about two Latinx girls, ages eight and ten. Did we want to meet them? the social worker asked. We can do that? we asked back. A preplacement visit was set up at the Department of Social Services for after the holidays. When I told my dad there'd be no children joining us at Christmas, he said, not unkindly, "Well, that's a relief."

The visit felt farcical from the start. We spotted the birth family in the government waiting room and tried communicating with them through our eyebrows. Look, we're not trying to take your kids! Truly, we're not sure we like kids! Smile, look away, gentle laugh, somber furrow. By the time all of us were called back, my facial muscles were tweaked.

A social worker escorted us through the light-filled atrium of soaring ceilings and suspended walkways. It reminded me of an airport, all the people gliding to and from, their baggage tucked under their skin instead of under their arms. When we finally arrived at our destination, a square office with glass walls on two sides, we took our seats. The introductions were brief, uneasy. One woman was identified as the girls' mother, the other a godmother who had been keeping the girls as part of a kinship placement for the last year. Another foster parent, there to meet the girls' six-year-old sister, rounded out our group of anxious travelers.

The social worker had instructed us to bring pictures of our house to show the girls. If you can believe it, the girls were in the room with us, too, during those first few impossible minutes. Youngest curled up under her mother's armpit and stared. Middle sobbed onto her godmother's firm shoulder. Oldest sat at a table by herself, now and then lifting her pink, kid glasses to rub her eyes. Somewhere in my chest, a heat both surprising and steady began to form, like the heat that spreads after you've raised your hand but before you're called on to answer.

The pictures seemed stupid now.

After the girls left, escorted off to another waiting room, another flight to the land of in-between, we exhaled. Now what? What were we here to learn? What are you supposed to ask to weigh if *your hypothetical, future child* is a fit? We didn't know. And so, I pulled a small, spiral notebook out of my oversized sweater and began asking questions without context, which are the only kinds of questions you can ask when life is teetering on the edge of the theoretical.

What do they like to eat?

Picky, their mom said through a translator.

When do they go to bed?

Whenever, their godmother answered in English.

How do they do with dogs?

This was our nonnegotiable. Others in the foster parent training had drawn the line over toddlers who threw poop or teens who talked back. Our worst-case scenario was jerks who kicked dogs.

They love dogs, their mom assured us, but Youngest had an allergic reaction to rabbits once.

Rabbits?

At this, the other prospective foster parent piped in. She had a rabbit! A rabbit who lived inside! She could bring the child home and see if she broke out in hives, but she'd hate to risk another move. What to do? she asked, one foot already pointed toward the door.

Does it surprise you that I thought first of the furniture—how we could fit one more bed, one more dresser, one more body into a 12' × 10' box? I was sure we could. And so it happened that I returned home from that preplacement visit and penned a zealous e-mail to the social worker saying, How do we start the paperwork to get licensed for three children instead of two?

I had spent so much of my adult life learning to conserve energy, and now all I could think of was how to spend it. I simply, as you well know, did not spend it imagining myself a mom.

IT TURNS OUT that other people were happy to imagine for me. No sooner were the three girls packed into the backseat of our compact car like sardines in puffy winter coats, when it started happening.

There was the first time a dental hygienist inquired, "Did you bring the insurance card, Mom?" I shot my arm out quickly, "You can call me Erin." *Mom* was so impersonal.

There was the first time my brother started a call with, "Hey, Moooom!" and I gasped, "How dare you. I am a *parent*." *Mom* was so presumptuous.

The first time I overhead Oldest mumble "my mom" when asked by a classmate who that White woman was hovering nearby, I decided it was time to call my therapist. *Mom* was so intimate.

And I was tired of being spooked.

An Answer from Mother Eve

"*Mom* is generally what we here in America call the parent sexed female," my therapist reassured me. But I am not generally persuaded by sentences with the word *generally* in them.

It's why I find myself, some years later, still trying to understand my specific grievance with the word *mom*, especially given that people had been so eager for me to become one.

The fanfare started even before I began parenting. I would tell friends and family that I was childfree, and they would assure me, as if it were due to some lack of confidence rather than conviction, "But you'd make a great mom!" I don't want to overstate how often this happened—people were not lining up to convince me—but it was regular and baseless enough to make me wonder, *What makes everyone so sure?* What makes everyone so sure that a woman is mom material, let alone great mom material, despite the fact that she may very well be capable of it?

Funny, when I think about the answer to this question, I think about my dad.

My dear dad thinks me capable of many things. And not just capable of them but capable of being exceptional at them. When I got an A- on a quiz, he wondered what I could do next time to improve. When I got my master's degree, he asked, Why not keep going for the PhD? When I said that Rush and I were happy enough, just the two of us, he said, "But you'd make a great mom," as though the same "if you can, you should" philosophy applied to my life as powerfully as it did his.

It makes me wonder now. What do A's, PhDs, and moms all have in common? For people like my dad, I suppose they represent the end of victory road, the sign of subject mastery, the crowning achievement in one's field of study. And that's it, isn't it? *Mom* is the crowning achievement in a woman's field of study. There's little that proves this point better for me than learning that Rachel Held Evans, bestselling author of *The Year of Biblical Womanhood*, was once turned down by a publisher who did not think she could write convincingly about womanhood without having experienced motherhood.[2]

Put simply, moms aren't just the summit of womanhood. They're the very definition of it.

PERSONALLY, I BLAME Eve for this false equivalence. Or to be clearer, I blame a common interpretation of the Eve story.

In the creation accounts of my tradition—and there are multiple—the sky is imagined as the palatial tent of the divine, Wisdom is pictured as a feminine presence who companions the Creator, and the Word is said to be both God and with God in the beginning. (If there is not a more regal creation story for a writer to embrace than this, someone tell me.) The book of Job is thought to house the oldest creation account of all. One could use any of these origin stories to understand the human story, but it's the Adam and Eve narrative that often looms largest in our collective imagination of what it means to be a woman: naturally relational, disastrously involved, and, most importantly, a mother.

The story starts like this.

In the beginning, there is an *us* God, as in "Let us make *adam* in our image . . . So God created *adam* in his image, in the image of God he created them, male and female he created them." Here, we have not only a *he* (or a *she*) God but a *we* God. The same pronoun could be used of the first *adam*, not yet a proper name but the Hebrew word translated as *man*, sometimes translated as *humankind*, literally translated *red*, like red clay, like red clay people. Again, not an Adam or an Eve human but a *we* human. Humanity, like divinity, is a community. Male and female, you could say, are but two stars in a constellation that hint at human wholeness and reflect God's gender-fullness.* ³

In another beginning, God puts a single *adam* in the Garden of Eden and, after a few idle days, declares "it's not good for *adam* to be alone." So, woman is fashioned out of now capital-A Adam's rib. Woman eats first of the fabled fruit. Woman is cursed to be ruled by her relationship to both childbirth and

---

* This interpretation relies on a literary device called merism, "a common Biblical figure of speech in which a whole is alluded to by some of its parts." We still use merism in our everyday language when we say, "I searched high and low," or "I moved heaven and earth." To search high and low is to say you searched all the heights in between; to move heaven and earth is to say you moved even the space beyond what you can see. While only the pairs are named—high and low, heaven and earth—the existence of more is implied. The aim of merism is to be inclusive, all-encompassing. So, when the biblical authors begin by saying God created night and day, dawn and dusk is implied. When the authors say God created birds and fish, lizards and turtles are implied. And when the authors say God created human beings male and female, all the expressions of sex between and beyond are implied. Humanity is meant to be inclusive, all-encompassing, like creation itself.

men. (Both, we're told, will be painful.) Directly on the heels of this not-so-pleasant pronouncement, Adam finally gives the woman her own name. She will be called Eve, we're told, "because she would become the mother of all living."

Um, is anyone else concerned that *woman* becoming synonymous with the word *mother* appears to be the result of a curse and not antecedent to it?

I don't wish to make too much of this textual timing. Martin Luther, of Protestant Reformation fame, certainly didn't. He believed that motherhood was part of God's perfect plan for women even before our fall from grace. "In the state of innocence, women would not only have given birth without pain, but their fertility would also have been far greater," he supposed. Nevertheless, Luther imagined Eve was comforted by the concessions of the curse. "She sees she is keeping her sex and that she remains a woman. She sees that she is not being separated from Adam to remain alone and apart from her husband. She sees that she may keep the glory of motherhood."[4] Eden has just been wrenched from our sorry hearts, but at least we are keeping our sex. Oh, bliss.

But, and I do promise I'm almost done with this particular bone, what if a woman is ultimately meant to be loved beyond her sex and not because of it?

There's good evidence to suggest that what's really Edenic is to exist without the possibility of motherhood at all. That's

right. No fertility. No infertility. No desire for children what-
soever. We see this most clearly in traditional Jewish and
Christian conceptions of the afterlife whereby one presumably returns to their most gorgeous and essential self.

For instance, in the Talmud, this future is imagined as a
world without hunger, without thirst, without childbirth. (I
know, for some of you, this future sounds awfully boring.)
Contrary to popular conceptions, here earthly desires are
not so much satisfied as they are sharpened. The presence of
God is the thing you have wanted all along, the thing you
are meant to want most, more than anything, more than
children.

The Bible, too, casts a vision in which embracing unity
with God, rather than social differences (like "Jew" or "Greek")
or biological differences (like "male" and "female"), is the
mark of spiritual maturity. Where once an individual's sex
may have been part of God's grand plan for humanity, with
the arrival of Jesus in human history, early Christians began
professing baptism, not babies, as the true sign of faith—and
a taste of the world to come.

These visions of the afterlife are, to be sure, a surprising
reversal of modern assumptions. It is not the childless who
are meant to ascend to motherhood. But mothers who are
meant to return to a state of childlessness. From a spiritual
vantage point, then, you might say that the childless represent
the end of victory road, the sign of subject mastery, the crowning achievement in humanity's field of study.

When I inform Janell of this possibility, she says, "Yeah, I've never heard that sermon on Mother's Day."

So, PERHAPS, THAT'S it then. It isn't the "generally" part of my therapist's definition that's been tripping me up. It's the "sexed female" part that's my beef with the word *mom*.

Now, truly, there is nothing wrong with being sexed female. If it isn't already obvious by now, *I am sexed female*, even if I am what you might call the "low femme" variety. Indeed, I very much like the company of others who identify as female, many of whom are also moms. But I am also intent on expanding our definition of a mom, of a woman for that matter, beyond body parts. I would very much like to live in a world where we care more about how a woman conceives of herself rather than how she fits into a pre-conceived box.

Conventionally speaking, I always thought I'd make a better dad than mom. The kind that arrives home from the office after five o'clock, loosens their yellowed collar, ruffles a kid's head before flopping into a recliner with a good book and a brown drink. This picture did not exactly fit my own dad, mostly because for much of my childhood, he did not hold a traditional job. He was a tireless self-starter, always launching another company with another name I would not remember.

It wasn't that I aspired to emulate men; though they did seem to enjoy more freedom than the women in their lives. It was that I recognized myself in these men: how they seemed happier leaning back than leaning in, the way they managed to spend their afternoons bantering instead of bent over the Corningware. I adored the women in my world even as I grew more and more curious about how to expand the notion of what a woman, and later a mom, looked like.

This was part of the strategy behind fostering, if you can call signing up to be a parent when you didn't really want to be a parent a strategy. Yes, it was an antidote to boredom. Yes, it was a vehicle for community. It was also a way to become a parent, unconventionally speaking. Because if I had to become a parent, if I really had to become a parent (I did not have to become a parent), then I would have to do it differently, entrepreneurially.

Of this much my dad would approve.

A Question for My Therapist, Part II

Sitting across from her, leaning back with legs crossed like my dad, I wanted to know, "So, what even *goes* in the mom box that wouldn't also go in the dad box?"

"Anything you do to care for your children," my therapist purred, which sounded like just the sort of beautiful, unusable thing I expected from her.

An Answer from Mother Dog

Amelia would always be our first kin. I draw the line at calling dogs fur babies because (1) dogs are not some imitation-crab version of children, and (2) it obscures how dogs so very often end up parenting us. I never minded being her mom, even as I accepted that with the girls' arrival, she had become mine.

Amelia barked at the girls, barked and jumped and bucked liked a baby bronco, when the girls came through the front door their first anxious evening. We had been over the plan with them on the car ride home from their elementary school: unpack, potato bar for dinner, go to the park. Middle, sensing our seriousness, interrupted, "Don't worry. We know how to have fun." By the time evening arrived and we pulled out Amelia's leash, they were so busy arguing over who got to walk her and for how long that they forgot to be sad for a while.

Everything was a negotiation in those early days. What would they call us? Rush and Erin was good enough, we agreed. What about our family values, a reasonable chore for a child, or—getting more basic now—a proper bedtime? Google said the universal favorite was eight. There were so many new routines to remember that the girls asked if we could type them up and print them out and post them on the fridge. I liked them even more with their shared belief that a pdf could solve anything.

Negotiating the division of labor proved trickier. How to share parenting in a culture that unfairly burdens—yet glorifies—moms? Fostering older kids who didn't see my body as a shelter or a meal had been a good start. Rush and I also made a pact that there'd be no "breadwinner privilege"; just because he made more money didn't mean his work had more value or mine was more easily dropped. The real boon was that as foster parents, we received government assistance; everything from the girls' medical bills to their after-school care was covered.

It turns out it's remarkably easy to be equitable when everyone's basic needs are met.

What else was there? We still had to decide who would be responsible for which tasks, so that neither of us, mainly me, would over-function. (I am very Eve-like in this way.) Money, groceries, medical stuff, and activity planning fell under my umbrella as the more, shall we say, visionary one. Maintenance, cooking, school stuff, and actually being able to stay 100 percent engaged through activities went to Rush as the more pragmatic one. Like stones in buckets, we dropped one responsibility in, and then another, until we felt like the weight was balanced, equally yoked, if you like.

The trouble is no one gives a damn about your invisible buckets. If a teacher wanted to schedule a meeting, it was my cell phone she called. No matter that we listed Rush as the primary contact. If a church member dropped off a meal, they'd sigh at how tired I must be. No matter that Rush had just spent twelve hours satiating the girls' appetite for the church social scene. It was Rush's name that was printed on the monthly checks from DSS. It was my name that rang from the girls' mouths every Saturday when all our well-intentioned weekday rhythms ran out. Sometimes even your children can be woefully old-fashioned.

It felt as if the whole world was conspiring for me to be what was convenient for them. Female Parent = Mom. Mom = Primary Caregiver. Primary Caregiver = All-Consuming-Love. All-Consuming-Love = Feminine. Feminine = Female Parent. It was an exhausting logic. The effort it took to offer a reframe for others was exhausting, too. "Feel free to call my husband about that." "Actually, I'm not worn out from being hands-on." "I promise you, girls, Rush is more proficient at ponytails."

On good days, I tried to remind myself that the world was as tired as I. Schoolteachers were not scheming my diminishment; they were underpaid, overworked treasures who no more had the bandwidth for every child to have an individualized education plan than they did for every adult to have one, too. On bad days, I hid under the duvet and pretended to be asleep whenever someone called my name.

Amelia called me *Mom*. By this, I mean Rush called me *Mom* and had been doing so for years in this scratchy, sort of cartoon voice. Ridiculous, I know. But it wasn't *really* Rush speaking, I told myself. It was Amelia, Amelia who punched guests with her paws, Amelia who sneered at groping hands, Amelia who groaned, dramatically, when spent. "She's bad at first impressions," I'd apologize to visitors, "but she'll grow on you." When I gave the spiel to our friend Chelsea, she shrugged and said, "I like a dog who likes some space." And, for a moment, it felt like maybe there was room for an ornery woman in the world, too.

The girls adored Amelia's voice, too. They loved when she gossiped about the neighborhood dogs, loved when she mocked Rush for his excessive use of the word *unacceptable*, loved her crass catchphrase, "Bitch, please," which was coincidentally also the name of her make-believe blog. They loved her, and they told her all the time. After returning home from school, they'd put their noses up to her nose, and through clenched teeth, say, "I love you, Amelia. I missed you, Amelia. Did you miss me, Amelia?" They didn't dare show such bald longing toward us. Instead, Amelia became their surrogate, too, a fistful of auburn fur into which they could bury their faces and fears.

Sometimes, a child's head resting heavy on her belly, I would catch Amelia watching me, her breath shallow and laboring, and think to myself, *I know, love.*

It's so much better to have a mom than to be a mom.

A Question for My Therapist, Part III

I knew what my therapist was getting at.

That I could just start going around the house and affirming that yes, when I did the budget, I was being a mom; when I researched what trauma does to the brain, I was being a mom; when I went to work on preparing a talk about the gender of God, I was being a mom; and so on and so on and so forth. Amelia had been teaching me as much.

"Okay. I hear you that I am *technically* the mom," I said

hurriedly, ever mindful of our ticking clock. It takes me so very long to tell the truth. "But doesn't the world have enough mothers?" Then, uncrossing my legs, "And what if I don't have the capacity to be one of them?"

"You may not," my therapist interrupted.

Now, this was more like the tough love I was paying for.

She went on, "But relationship grows capacity."

Oh, dear.

An Answer from Revolutionary Mothers

"You know it's the *but* part of the 'you'd make a great mom' compliment that gets to me," a childfree friend says. "It's like they haven't listened to a word I've said. If they're genuinely worried about encouraging me, I'd rather them just ask, 'Honey, do you doubt yourself?'"

She has a point, though I'm not entirely sure how I would have answered this question had anyone asked before I became a parent. Of course I doubted myself; didn't most people to some degree? But doubt was no more a reason to do something than it was not to do something. Doubt was the soundtrack to being alive. It's what made you human. It's what made you not a narcissist. Since when were we not allowed to have or heed our doubts?

I doubted that parenting was good for the creative life, my creative life, which benefited from both a closed door and an open day. I doubted that parenting, at least the biological kind, was good for my body, good for my neighbor, good for my mental health, which wavered even in the best of circumstances. I did not believe that honoring these limits was the same thing as "settling" for an A- or a master's degree.

And, yes, I doubted that I would make a great mom, not because I was *terribly* insecure, but because I didn't think I made for a good woman, conventionally speaking, and the one had always seemed prerequisite for the other.

But the truth is I *did* make for a good woman on a few important fronts. And it wasn't by being naturally relational or disastrously involved. It was by being perceived as competent (read: "formally educated"). It was by being perceived as steadfast (read: "legally married"). It was by being perceived as the picture of piety (read: White, heterosexual, and Christian). I can only assume that a good deal of the confidence in my would-be mothering skills came from the projection of these particular qualities rather than any proof of caregiving capacity.

When I listed my shortcomings to others—for instance, did you know that it actually angers me when Rush catches a cold, or that my personal bubble is the size of the Universal Studios globe?—they did not want to hear it. They emphasized, "You are so *intentional*," as if intentions alone could cover over a theme park's worth of vice.

So, WHEN I come across this quotation on social media one morning—"What would it mean for us to take the word *mother* less as a gendered identity and more as a possible action . . . ?"—I think to myself, *hallelujah.*[5]

The book from which the quotation comes arrives in the mail a few days later, crisp, orange, velvety to the touch. When I peel back its cover, *Revolutionary Mothering* turns out to be as revolutionary as it sounds. Piece after piece in the anthology speaks to the need not to abandon the word *mother* but to radicalize it. This is the work Black women have long taken up in the wake of state violence, forced sterilization, and soul-sucking stereotypes that don't just bruise but kill: to transform *mother* from a noun that reproduces the status quo into a verb that subverts it.

Already, I like the sound of this.

I am especially drawn to an essay from editor Alexis Pauline Gumbs, who describes a very different feeling than mine when told she'd make a great mom. She was surprised. Both Black and queer, Gumbs had wanted to become a mother, even dreamed of becoming a mother, but it had never occurred to her that it was something to celebrate. She explains, "I have been taught that mothering is something that happens to you, and you deal with it, and fight for it, swallowing down shame and living with the threat that the state wants nothing more than to take your kids away from you in every way imaginable."

In all my years of resistance to the reassurance, it never occurred to me that the compliment could feel not just novel but welcome for some women.

I can see now that there are a number of reasons I've been hesitant about the category of mom—the generalization of women in it, the feminization of women in it—but there's also the exclusion of some women from it. The instant recognition of me as "Mom" when we started fostering felt like an instant erasure of the woman our girls called "Mami." I could tell the girls felt this way, too, the way their shoulders rolled forward and their eyes darted down when someone called me by her name. It was like the fissure of their family had already been written. It was like people were rooting for me, not her. If she received the same government payments to raise her kids that we do now, surely she wouldn't be called a saint but a drain on the system.

So, I'm starting to get it. For Gumbs to be told she'd make a great mom in a country where people who are Black, Brown, Indigenous, poor, disabled, and queer have had to fight for their rights to parent *is* revolutionary. But for women like me who have historically been granted motherhood's mantle? Well, there's nothing special in being told we'd excel at what's expected of us. The revolution, I'm gathering, is to love in ways that are not expected of us.

But what does that look like?

I think of Jessica, a friend with a physical disability who mothers her adoptive son with an attentiveness I could never sustain. (You will not meet a woman with more patience for toddler blabber.) She writes, because she is also a gorgeous writer, "My love isn't diminished by my inability to carry my son up the stairs, just as it isn't diminished by the fact that I didn't carry him inside my uterus."[6] In a world that worships mom-bods as the epitome of superhuman strength, her body offers an alternative model of care in which presence is prized over performance.

Then there's Shalom, a friend who mothers two White stepchildren with the same thirst for justice she has for her biological child. (She is not, for the record, as enamored as I am with children calling her by her first name. Honorifics were a big deal in her Filipino upbringing.) In a world that segregates the ultimate concerns of one racial group from another, her household offers a different vision of community, one in which "the liberation of my child is bound up in the liberation of all children," she says.

My friend Becky is embracing a kind of mothering, too. She's mothering herself after coming out as an adult to her conservative Cuban parents. "I'm learning I don't have to be the kind of woman anybody else thinks I should. I can just do my thing to make good in this world and bring heaven on earth and love hard and fail hard and live honestly. And none of that is about children, which is bizarre, given my upbringing." In a world that preaches real women are mothers and real mothers are conventionally feminine, her self-love offers another route to repair.

It is, of course, impossible (and tiring) to be revolutionary all the time. But, at the very least, we can temper our faith in the "good woman" equals "great mom" equation. Gloria

Steinem, a childless woman who mothered the American feminist movement, summed it up perfectly once: "As a noun, *mother* may be good or bad, willing or unwilling, on welfare or rich, worshipped or blamed, dominating or nurturing, accidental or chosen . . . / But when *mother* is a verb—as in *to mother, to be mothered*—then the best of human possibilities come into our imaginations."

Linguistically, it is a nearly imperceptible shift, from mother as a noun to mother as verb. And, in the days after discovering it, there are still questions, questions not unlike the ones that plagued me and my kindly therapist some years ago. ("But what even counts as mothering that wouldn't also count as fathering?") Still, there is a fluidity to the shift, which suits me. Mothering becomes practice, not status. Motion, not emotion. Capacity, not identity.

WHILE CONSIDERING MY relationship to mothering afresh, I'm mildly pleased by how certain capacities of mine have grown. For example, while Rush continues to receive all school communications and attend all school meetings, I once made an appearance in Youngest's classroom on career day. ("What kind of stuff do you write about?" a child asked. "True stuff?" I answered.) However, the word *mom*, common or proper, still feels imperfect. I still prefer to be called a parent. I still prefer to be called Erin.

One of the rituals that remains from our first few moons

of fostering is the practice of praying over dinner. Each person is assigned to lead one weekday night. A sauce-splattered blessing book sits nearby with prayers Christian and Jewish, Hindu and Buddhist, Islamic and Native American. I can still remember when their small mouths struggled to sound out the words: *bounty, countenance, shineth*. We needed ready-made prayers in those days, which is, of course, still these days. So, I taught them the Lord's Prayer, changing the words slightly from the ones I learned growing up: "Our Mother, who art in heaven, hallowed be thy name."

I do not pray this way because I think God is a Mother any more than God is a Father. (Remember, not a *he* or a *she* God but a *we* God.) No, I pray this way because I think titles for God are best when they, like mothering, disrupt us, expand us. Sometimes still, while hiding from the girls under the duvet, a shame I thought I'd long outwitted finds me. It's hard to say if this shame is just part of the territory of being an imperfect parent, or if it's more specifically located in the experience of being an imperfect woman. I'm inclined to believe the latter. And so there is something infinitesimally weird and wonderful about using a title for God that I am not entirely comfortable using of myself.

I am not always capable of being a mother.

But I think God is.

I think, together, *we* are.

Titles may be who I am to you but names are who I am to myself. The first time God utters God's name it is a name as gargantuan and inclusive as being itself: "I am who I am." Pastor Lisa once shared her favorite translation of this phrase with me: "I will be who you need me to be." It is a name both self-liberating and self-giving. It is name that says it doesn't matter what you call me but that you can count on me. I like this so very much that I resolve to tell the girls the same.

Call me whatever you want but I'm yours.

A Small Miracle

One Saturday afternoon, not long after my fateful trip to the therapist, I took the girls to a petting zoo. Another foster parent had told me the place was magical. She took her kid here to pet bunnies. (Youngest was *not*, mysteriously, miraculously, allergic.) Petting bunnies sounded like a good way to whittle the day.

Winterpast Farm was the kind of place where flies go to feast. On apple rot off a goat's beard. Or dung from a miniature donkey. Children wandered around serving bottomless baskets of feed as if they were waiters at an Olive Garden. When we got out of the car, the dust was thick enough to lick.

A woman with rainbow hair waved us in. This was the Farmer Mary I had read about on the website. Farmer Mary adopted two of her four children. Text Farmer Mary before coming. Farmer Mary does not have change.

First the emu, then the pigs. The girls walked the property like a labyrinth, slowly, methodically. Perhaps they sensed that we were not so much as killing time here but metering it out, minute by minute, pellet by pellet. We saved the bunnies for last. Oldest crowded their cages, waiting her turn, mouth open but mute.

"Where is your adult?" Farmer Mary asked her.

And for the first time in three months she did not flinch when she pointed to me. She was not asked to betray her mom by calling me "Mom." She got to claim a grown-up who was with her and for her but needed little from her.

For the first time since we arrived, the sucking flies sounded like birdsong.

An unassuming word, in the truest sense: Adult. The Adult. Your Adult.

Our Adult, who art in Heaven, hallowed be thy name.

A small miracle, caught in the sieve of an endless Saturday.

CHAPTER 5

Script: Children Are a Gift from God

Rewrite: Pleasure Is a Pretty Great Gift, Too

Inloveness is a gift of the gods,
but then it is up to the lovers to cherish or to ruin.
—SHELDON VANAUKEN[1]

I WAS ON the birth control pill for a crippling case of menstrual cramps when I first met Rush.

It hardly mattered; both of us had committed to saving the baby-making kind of sex for our future spouses. This was an important tenet from our youths—he the lifelong Methodist and I, already, the lapsed Catholic. It was also an important tenet of the many fervent campus groups who preached that abstinence now would make for hot, godly sex later.

I don't remember anyone preaching what came after the hot, godly sex part; as future sexperts, we would be left to discern on our own questions of if and when we'd try for children, if and what kind of family planning we'd use, and what level of human interventions we'd be comfortable with when it came to our fertility.

Rush was small, dark-skinned, snaggletoothed. The first time I saw him carrying a tray through the cafeteria, the universe blurred, he came into focus, and there is no other way to explain it. As if to assure him that there is no other way to explain it, I tell him, "I mean, you are attractive but not that attractive."

When he leaned across library tables, Rembrandt or Rothko books fanned out in front of him, a slip of hairy midriff sometimes showed; that slip undid me. When we'd watch movies on one of those combo TV/VCR devices in my dorm room, just touching his doughy little palms sent a heat wave through me. And, oh, we could talk. Eighteen years old and not yet prone to falling asleep, I could stay up for hours philosophizing with him.

I had asked him out on our first date, and he had not balked. Rush says he found my intensity exciting, my candor charming. I wouldn't describe it as a traditionally "kid-friendly" combination, highly cerebral and with a low tolerance for noise. He, on the other hand, spoke plainly, laughed loudly. We met at a coffee shop, when I didn't drink coffee, and talked for five hours on a raging, winter day. I felt like melted butter in a measuring bowl. I could safely lose my shape with him.

After three years of dating, he agreed to marry me on the condition that I may never want children; he wasn't sold on them, either. This surprised me. This still surprises me. He appeared to be a man marked by tradition.

There were the "yes, ma'ams" and "no, sirs" that rolled off his tongue as sweet as Southern dinner buns.

There was the stained-glass necklace he wore, a relic from the church he grew up in, and I do mean grew up *in* and not *going to*; his parents had rented the abandoned chapel off Main Street.

There was also the curious fact that when we got engaged the fall of my senior year, he said he wanted me to take his last name because "I've always imagined it that way." (I obliged before legally returning to my birth name four years later; "I forget why it mattered so much to me," he says now with a shrug.)

He was sentimental through and through, and yet he imagined little in the way of parenting. He didn't have to. A young man didn't have to account for how fatherhood would fit his life the same way a young woman did hers.

Rush and I agreed to premarital counseling sessions with not one but two pastors. We were smug about it, too, how there was no laundry we could not air together. We talked shared families, shared finances, even shared intimacy. But neither pastor, to my recollection, talked to us about shared contraception.

In the fog of this theological silence, I turned to my mother, the nurse, for medical guidance. Until there was a male equivalent of the birth control pill, we decided I would stay on the female version and Rush would not balk at buying the menstrual products.

We agreed to reevaluate our decision in five years and then, at the five-year mark of marriage, quickly agreed to another five.

The Altar of Good

Rush and I had been married a mostly happy six years when I published my first book, an anthology I coedited in which I'd also supplied an essay on being married without children. It was the first time I'd ever publicly floated the phrase "child-free for the common good" to describe Rush's and my way of life, and you could say I was more than mildly pleased with it.

As a flourishing end to the piece, I thought it noble, strategic even, to use the language of conservatives to make my point that "the survival of the human race depends on sacrifices of many sorts, made for the good of all and the love of God."

The trouble, I'd come to learn, is that conservatives do not allow for this particular kind of sacrifice. The pastor of the evangelical church I attended at the time cursed contraceptive devices for allowing children to be picked up and put down like hobbies. *What was a hobby?* I wondered, my arms in permanent "Thriller" position from typing theology papers. Then there was Pope Francis, countercultural though he may have been driving around Rome in his humble Ford Focus, who famously chastised childfree couples for privileging a life of travel, leisure, and pets.[2] As if we were one bougie monolith.

This pro-natalism perplexed me, particularly coming from the Pope. Catholic tradition has long supported *single* men and women who were willfully celibate. There was Jesus, of course, who purportedly never married, never made babies, and toured around town with a band of twelve male disciples and "some women." The Apostle Paul picked up where Jesus left off in commending the bachelor life. However, ever the pragmatic, he allowed that marriage was a viable, if not concessionary, option for those who couldn't quiet their desires otherwise.

As theologian Dale Martin points out in his book *Sex and the Single Savior,* much of the ancient world believed that marriage was largely for the purpose of lawful procreation. But such procreation—the kind that produced legitimate heirs— was necessary only in light of one's impending death. And if Jesus conquered the grave, so to speak, then what was the point of reproducing? "For the historical Jesus," Martin argues, "the rejection of marriage and the family was as necessary as the proclamation of the resurrection and the eternal kingdom of God."[3] It was tricky to embrace one without undermining the other.

How then, you ask, did Christians get the reputation for being the marriage-and-family-values people? Good question.

Jesus may have conquered the grave, but his followers did not. Not literally, at least. According to tradition, Paul was beheaded. Peter was crucified. James was clubbed to death. John, to whom Jesus assigned the care of his own mother, was the only disciple thought to have died from old

age. Amidst this ancient tumult, some biblical authors, perhaps feeling like they had to account for the ongoing usefulness of the household, positioned the hierarchy of the home
(man, woman, child, slave—in that order) as a model for the
gathered church.[4]* To be clear, this was an alternative point
of view to the Gospel narratives, and for more than fifteen
hundred years, remained the minority opinion. To put a finer
point on it, when a Roman Christian named Jovian argued at
the end of the fourth century that those who married and had
sex were simply no worse in the eyes of God than those who
remained single and celibate, he and eight of his friends were
excommunicated.

Not until the sixteenth century did King Henry VIII's desire to end his own marriage spark an emphasis on all marriages across England and beyond. Denied an annulment by
the Pope in a country already seeded with anti-Catholicism,
Henry closed monasteries throughout the land and opened
the door to clerical marriage. The figure of the priest as holy
man was replaced by the parson as family man. Seventeenth-
century Puritans, convinced these reforms were not enough
and facing persecution from Church and Crown, took this
new focus on the family one step further and made their

---

* The famous Christian "household codes," found in the biblical books of Ephesians,
Colossians, and 1 Timothy, although written in the name of the Apostle Paul are thought
by many scholars to be written after his death. The same goes for the epistle 1 Peter and
its pseudonymous author Peter. However, as scholar Sharyn Dowd argues, the biblical
authors "advocated this system not because God had revealed it as the divine will for
Christian homes, but because it was the only stable and respectable system anyone knew
about." Put simply, Dowd says, "It was the best the [Greco-Roman] culture had to offer."

homes into "separate," "pure," and "holy" households. No longer was the home a model for the church, but now the home *was* the church, that is, the real site of religious activity. These were the same Puritans, mind you, who would take their practices to the New World and pass them on to generations of Americans, many of whom now believe that the family is a God-ordained institution in need of defending.

So, there you have it, in obscenely broad brushstrokes, how the leaders of a religion known for its critique of marriage and sex decided that they needed marriage and sex for their survival.

What about those Catholics, though? Did they at least hold on to the ideal of holding out? Well, yes and no.

By the mid-twentieth century the Catholic Church was trying to remain steadfast in a changing world. Among these changes were population growth in much of the Global South and the legalization of birth control in much of the Global North. So, the Pope did what church folk do best. He gathered a committee to examine the issues. The result was an encyclical published in 1968 called "Humanae Vitae," in which Pope Paul VI reaffirmed the Church's traditional position that sex was "ordained toward" procreation. But the Pope also professed a position agreeable to more modern sensibilities, though long supported by scriptures; sex was meant to be "unitive," too, a self-giving glue between spouses.

You could almost hear the progressives hold their breath. If sex wasn't *only* for the purpose of procreation, could that open the door for faithful expressions of intimacy among childfree couples, same-sex couples, unmarried couples, self-loving solo-artists? The answer was no. The dual purposes of sex were inseparable in the eyes of the Church. Which meant any form of sex that was not at least *open* to the transmission of life within marriage was condemned. Which meant artificial birth control remained off-limits. The Pope was clear. "It is never lawful, even for the gravest reasons, to do evil that good may come of it."[5]

In other words, "childfree for the common good" had always been dead on arrival.

I wish I could report to you that I have always been impervious to what the Pope thinks of me. (To be sure, I didn't know what the Pope thought of me until more recently.) Or that I know better than to put my worth in the hands of pastors who preach a puritanical God. (Apparently, this God is deeply invested in marriage retreats.) The only explanation I can offer now is that sometimes I like to worship at the same altar of good behavior that my critics do.

Before the publication of my first book, I hadn't really grasped the moral argument against couples without children. Nor did I grasp why *my* moral argument was in some ways equally problematic. Did I really believe that sacrifice was the best use of sex, procreative or otherwise? Or had I only said that to prove a point, that I am just as capable of piety as parents, that truthfully hobbies have never come naturally to me?

Not until I read my essay aloud to a women's group at my

local church did I see the error. An older woman raised her hand during the question-and-answer time. "You say being childfree is a sacrifice as worthy as parenting," she started, "but sacrifice isn't why I decided to have children. It was pleasure. Because I wanted to, and I thought I'd enjoy it." She waited for a response. But my thoughts felt like marshmallow, puffy and hard to pull apart.

Was she telling me that some people actually admitted to doing things out of pleasure and not piety? That some people didn't think they had to prove themselves before enjoying themselves? Was it possible that pleasure could be an altar of the holy, too?

Now *that* I had not seriously considered.

The Altar of Pleasure

What I had seriously considered, before marrying, was the weight of bearing children.

And why shouldn't a woman? It is her body at greater risk. So, if she has sex with a man, she will be the one more likely to use contraception. So, if she gets pregnant by a man, she will be the one more likely to make reproductive decisions. So, if she gives birth and is married to a man, she will be the one more likely to opt out of paid work—and all the financial protections that come with it. Along the way, she will disproportionately bear the cost of both making and defending her choices no matter how traditional or progressive those choices might be. (Notably, over a third of births in the United States do not arise from conscious choice at all.[6]) Children are a gift, we insist, without admitting that for women, in particular, it is a gift of some consequence.

Sobering research aside, however, there was another reason, though it didn't feel like reason enough, that children might not be the gift for me: I'm not sure I enjoyed them when I was one of them. If given the choice, I chose to sit at the adult's table. If asked to babysit, I asked how long the child could sleep. (More than once, an employer returned to find me asleep.) A keen awareness accompanied me on school field trips; whenever we went someplace I'd already been— the zoo, the museum, Six Flags—I grew impatient, irritated even, with the other children who were pressing their face up to the glass for the first time. I was not interested in experiencing the same place through new eyes. I was interested in experiencing new places through my eyes, and for some reason, as I got older, that felt to me like a qualitatively different joy than the one I heard parents describe.

However, dismissing children as a category is, I've learned, either very uncommon or very unpopular or very both nowadays. But is it immoral? C. S. Lewis—a stepparent without progeny of his own—thought that to delight in children was part and parcel of knowing the *Tao* or the "objective value" of some things. Along with venerable old men (he makes no mention of storied old women), children possess a quality that he said, "*demands* a certain response from us whether we make it or not."[7] Although Lewis confessed that he, like me, did not "enjoy the society of small children,"[8] he saw that as a defect in himself rather than mere preference.

But exactly what quality makes children so special, and whether anyone else possesses it—shouldn't we be delighting in all human beings?—is still unclear to me. If I were to guess, I might call this preferential quality "vulnerability" and the preferential people who possess it the poor, the orphan, the widow, the prisoner, the outcast. That there are some of us who do not delight in children should not worry us as much as the fact that there are some of us who are not moved by human need, our own included. Children are one kind of vulnerable, and often only for a time, and some more than others.

I fell in love with Rush when I was barely more than a child myself. I had dated some in high school. There were All-American baseball boys, theater boys with English accents, one college boy who liked to punch other boys at parties. But I decided I was too much, too dark, for them. I decided they were too little, too light, for me. I decided I'd rather a best friend than a boyfriend. So, it felt like a rare joy to find both in the same body, even rarer to find a man who didn't want a mother but a wife and not just a wife but a partner. "You're lovely, but I wish I'd met you at thirty," I told Rush, embarrassed by all my new and off-brand happiness.

By the time Rush and I were engaged, it was clear that if a rich, intimate partnership was what we wanted most, then children had to be carefully weighed, especially in twenty-first-century America where a strange mix of family-friendly values and family-hostile policies made it hard for parents to thrive as equals. I was sure some brave souls figured it out. But I didn't have good reason to chance it. If we lived in France, and worked some land together, and there were colorful chickens to occupy the children, then *maybe*, I conceded.

I had never heard anyone put it similarly until my senior year of college, when a friend handed me Sheldon Vanauken's spiritual memoir, *A Severe Mercy*. Vanauken and his wife, Davy—friends of C. S. Lewis, actually—went from pagan partners to Christian lovers all while maintaining an intense, playful, and "willfully sterile" romance. It astounded me. Here was another couple so committed to a "unitive" intimacy that they believed it necessary to refuse the procreative kind. Of their decision not to have children, Vanauken wrote, "If children could be raised by a nanny, we sharing them for a few hours each day, or even if we were farmers, children might be a good. But in the pattern of modern life, where they became the centre for the woman, they were separating. We would not have children."[9]

Lewis, unsurprisingly, believed this to be a fool's errand. Every life was necessarily a solitary one. No one could live their lives in complete unison with another. Speaking from a heterosexist point of view, Lewis countered, "The conjugal act itself depends on opposite, reciprocal and therefore unshare-able experiences. Did you want her to feel she had a *woman* in bed with her?"[10]

No, Rush and I did not want to be sexual replicas of each other. But we wanted a marriage more than a child and thought it too treacherous to tempt biological parenting pulling us apart. It never occurred to us that this sort of scenario—marriage without children—could be construed as "having your cake and eating it, too." That, in the words of Lewis, a couple was not meant to "live to itself" any more than an individual was.[11] That there was something indulgent about hoarding all that pleasure.

Now, maybe it's because pleasure is not a talent of mine that I find the insinuation that Rush and I were hoarding too much of it in our non-procreative sex life laughable. If you must know, after our wedding day, I found sexual intercourse to be tender, predictable, painful. "Tilted pelvis," the nurse practitioner declared. There were positions we could try to ease the awkward geometry, but they were not nearly as thrilling as the ones from the Kama Sutra book my sister-in-law had gifted me upon my engagement.

This turn of events was disappointing but not devastating. Rush and I may not have enjoyed the "hot, godly sex" as advertised to faithful virgins, but we had years of exploring other facets of our partnership. Ironically, it was because we'd treated sexual intercourse as the pinnacle of intimacy for so long that we'd developed a number of satisfying alternatives to avoid it. These came in handy. He put me into my pajamas at night. I kissed his doughy little palms.

To be sure, there were times in those early years that I thought our marriage too precious for children, and times I thought it too volatile. There were times I was able to enjoy our non-procreative sex and times I thought I could do without sex entirely. (I wondered, would this appease the naysayers if I agreed to a willfully celibate marriage?) As we approached our eight-year anniversary, we asked what new challenges we could take on and how we might flex those muscles together. Rush's desire to become a foster parent felt just as surprising to me as his desire not to become a biological one. Here, we hoped, was a way to be generative without being separated.

So, perhaps we weren't exactly childfree for the common good after all. Perhaps we were childfree for our good pleasure.

Good Pleasure

"Humanae Vitae" had reasoned that children were not just a gift to the world but "the supreme gift of marriage" and contributed "in the highest degree to their parents' welfare." However, this was not exactly borne out in the books I pored over in my college sociology courses. It is not borne out in the books I pore over now. Marriage itself is a better predictor of life satisfaction than motherhood.[12] Within marriage, marital satisfaction, sex frequency, and affection have all been shown to be higher for couples without kids.[13] And while mental health varies greatly among parents, and over the course of parenthood, researchers have found that "there is no type of parent who reports less depression than nonparents."[14] When I share this information with a dad friend, he tells me, "Parental happiness studies are overrated." "I don't know," I tell him, "less depression sounds cool."

Thankfully, since the invention of reliable contraception, some denominational leaders have publicly affirmed that couples can responsibly enjoy the gift of marriage, and sex, without also receiving the gift of children.

Two years before "Humane Vitae," the General Assembly of the United Presbyterian Church (USA) put out a publication called "Sexuality and the Human Condition" that urged both married and unmarried couples to consider how their reproductive choices impacted their whole community, affirming "that God has put into our hands incredibly more effective and exact knowledge of the process of conception, including its control."[15]

Population control was chief among the concerns of Katharine Jefferts Schori, then the presiding bishop of the Episcopal Church, when she gave a controversial interview with the *New York Times*. Asked if her denomination wasn't interested in replenishing its ranks via reproduction (she mentioned that Catholics and Mormons had theological reasons for doing so), she replied, "No. It's probably the opposite. We encourage people to pay attention to the stewardship of the earth and not use more than their portion."[16]

Many rabbis have long allowed for the use of responsible contraception, reflecting a commitment to both the sanctity of life and a woman's quality of life. Recently, the Central Conference of American Rabbis affirmed a fifty-year history of opposing legislation that would impinge upon a woman's right to "weigh the tradition" alongside "her own personal decision" when it came to matters of healthcare, birth control, and abortion.[17]

Still, though plenty of people have made the argument that contraception honors life, the term *pro-life* remains the province of those who oppose reproductive interventions like birth control or, more often, abortion. I've often wondered if this isn't conservatives' main fear of the childfree: that we're all sex-crazed, leisure-seeking, abortion-having hobbyists.

But this is the great fiction: The childfree are not a monolith any more than conservatives are. On both sides, if you want to even call it sides, there can be pleasure and piety, there can be ambivalence and certainty, there can be grief and relief, there can be hard realities and fragile hopes, there can be choice *and* life.

TAKE KAREN, FOR instance. Karen is a fifty-five-year-old Southern Baptist who stopped using the birth control pill in her twenties over concerns that it didn't align with her

pro-life convictions. She and her husband believed in being "open to the transmission of new life," as the Catholics
would say, and then eventually started actively hoping for it.
It didn't happen. Karen was diagnosed with endometriosis.
She received treatment—"we don't disavow medicine," she
assures—but the couple drew the line at additional interventions like fertility drugs. They felt like this would create more
ethical dilemmas. They felt like their fate was up to God. It
wasn't their place to force open doors that God had closed.

Then there's Melody. Melody is a forty-one-year-old Muslim who grew up putting her faith in love, justice, and choice.
She explains, "You can't be a Muslim without choice. The
Qur'an specifically says, 'There shall be no compulsion in
religion.'" While her college classmates were dreaming about
their future weddings, she was dreaming about prosecuting
Milosevic at the Hague. In the parking lot of a Chuck E.
Cheese, she warned her future husband that she never wanted
children. She never wanted an abortion either; but she'd
mapped out her route to the closest clinic, should a pregnancy
occur. When guests at their wedding reception offered a
Insha'Allah (meaning *God willing*, next you'll have children),
she replied with a *Khoda nakoneh* (meaning, *God forbid*, I
don't).

Karen tells me she was open to biological children, but
when it came to the possibility of adopted ones, never felt
the circumstance was right. She bemoans the "birth control

mentality" that puts convenience over commitment, and yet she, too, is making choices about which lives she's obligated to privilege; we all are.

Melody doesn't want biological children but is quick to explain that it's not because she has bipolar disorder. (People are quick to assume she doesn't want to pass her "defect" on to progeny.) "God forbid" she gets pregnant, she says, but also "God forbid" we selectively rid the world of people with different abilities in our quest for genetic "perfection."

On first listen, Karen's and Melody's stories may sound worlds apart. They did to me. A Southern Baptist and a mystical Muslim. Pro-life and pro-choice. Infertile and intentionally so. And yet, the more I mull over them, the more I hear their big, generous, overlapping questions.

What reproductive choices make me feel human—like, finite, fragile, but also accountable?

What reproductive choices are accessible or allowable—according to my faith, my family, or my community?

What reproductive choices cause joy to flourish—for me, my people, all people?

These are the answers that good pleasure is after, and in the absence of more generous conversations from our communities—too many of whom focus on a strict (hetero) sex code before marriage but go mute on the ethics of reproduction writ large—I love how they acknowledge that questions of *if*, *when*, and *how* many children need some working

out, both personally and collectively and, yes, sometimes linguistically.

SO, I'VE TAKEN to defining good pleasure as this: a pleasure
that seeks what *feels* good alongside what *yields* good. Surely
this paradox is obvious to some of you. It is obvious that pleasure should cause flourishing. Or that being considerate can
be pleasurable. One needn't be sacrificed for the other.

Sacrifice, I understand now, is a ponderous word.

Recently, I found myself on a solo retreat at a sprawling
Franciscan prayer center in the woods. As if the two-bedroom
monastic cottage a few months prior was not luxurious enough,
now I had the happy embarrassment of shuffling around the
cavity of a four-bedroom one named after Saint Clare of
Assisi, founder of the Order of the Poor Ladies. Would St.
Clare approve of all this excess—excess space, excess joy? I
hoped so.

I'd driven two hours from home to reconnect. With my
surroundings. With my knowing. With my body. For three
days, I wandered the pine-needle paths and put my hand to
my chest and asked, "Yes, love?" I wrote in the morning
and did yoga in the afternoon and watched Netflix in the
evenings—because contemplation has its limits. I did not expect to reconnect with my childhood faith.

On the last night of my retreat, over a big bowl of salad
with dressing as viscous as glue, I shared a meal with an octo-

genarian priest in the communal dining hall. He appeared slight of build, relaxed in layers of pale skin. He had the unhurried gestures of a man who had done this all before, pushed his walker down the long, carpeted hallway, passed salt to a stranger in search of absolution.

Our exchange was friendly, calm. I told him I have three adopted girls. He told me, like everybody, how wonderful. I told him he wouldn't think it wonderful if he knew my story. After telling him my story (an abbreviated version), he told me it sounds like I've worked it out with God. "You know in your heart," he said, plainly, pushing aside a crouton. "You don't need a priest to bless your decision."

No, I suppose not. But given that a priest, and not only a priest but the Pope, had cursed this particular decision, I would take whatever non-blessing the Church owed me. I would take it, and I would put it in my pocket, and after a short, drizzly walk back to St. Clare's cottage, I would put it on the page, for anyone else to borrow.

A Gift Best Shared

Not long after returning home from my solo woodland retreat, I decide it's time to have my annual "body conference" with the girls. We get into our bathing suits, I drain some ginger ale into plastic cups, and Youngest grabs the bag of Epsom salts with her two hands and pours liberally into the lukewarm tub water.

When the younger girls have splashed around as long as I can stand, Oldest perched on the perimeter with me, I launch in.

It seems I've become a sexpert, after all.

"First, your body belongs to you and is designed for your pleasure," I start.

At the word *pleasure*, Oldest turns pink. I know there's more to the story of who bodies belong to and what bodies are made for than this, but given that they are young girls, shy girls who still wear biking shorts under their pleated skirts, this is a place to begin: by telling them that they get the say in what feels good, and feeling good is sacred.

"Second, sex with a partner is best between consenting adults," I continue on, before pausing to take a sip of soda.

This phrase is as imperfect as the first. But given the girls' history, given marriage's ambivalent history, I am more concerned with preaching consent than chastity. I am more concerned with emphasizing "how they love not who they love," as my friend Iris once put it so beautifully.

The third and last thing I tell the girls is this: "If and when you have sex, it's your responsibility to choose protection." I shift my weight.

Yes. It's an uncomfortable cleft we live in, between the things that happen to us and the things that happen with us. Not every pregnancy is a gift. Not all childlessness is a choice. But I want my girls to know that the call is not to erase or inflate our sense of agency. It's to be faithful in the sliver we've been given.

As the girls enter their teen years and their questions become more nuanced, more private to them, Rush and I may not be their safe place for all things sex. Which is why, in the midst of admiring our belly rolls up close, I make all three of them name one adult, other than their doctor, that they can confide in when the time comes.

"And if you are not ready to talk about having sex, then you are not ready to be having it," I say sternly, hoping to impress upon them the solemnity of the situation, as much as one can in a bikini.

And then, so I don't forget, so they don't forget, I write all of this down, including the names of the adults they can trust, in a binder that lives in our book-lined dining room.

Because of this much I'm sure: If children are a gift, they are a gift best shared.

CHAPTER 6

Script: It'll Be Different with Your Own

Rewrite: It's Extraordinary Who Can Become Your Own

> *The sphere of a wise woman is beyond herself, beyond her family, beyond the human community, embracing the planet, mothering the earth.*
>
> —ROBIN WALL KIMMERER[1]

OUR FIRST SPRING as foster parents, we signed the girls up for swim lessons at the downtown YMCA.

As a rule, we tried not to impose our cultural preferences on them. But water safety was a nonnegotiable for Rush, who comes from a family of beach fanatics. My nonnegotiable was Spanish classes. If given a choice of electives, they had to choose Spanish every time until they were fluent. We weren't fluent. And I worried. I worried about not being able to speak to their family when we needed all the family we could get—within reason.

I shouldn't have loved those swim lessons as much as I did. The humidity of the human-sized aquarium. The smell of chlorine on soggy bodies. The aggressive ridge of the bleachers beneath my bottom. But week after week, it was a forty-minute respite from being the responsible one, the one they called for, the one they asked of, the one they looked to.

Solitude was what I missed most after the girls moved in. Even when I took a glass of rosé into my office and shut the door and told them through wobbly panes of glass that "I will be out in an hour," there was still the feeling of being *on*. Thomas Merton, the American Trappist monk, once wrote that the true contemplative could find solitude anywhere, everywhere, no matter the noise or crowd.

But I decided that Merton must not have been a caregiver, not one of *the* caregivers, certainly not one of *the* caregivers who had recently diagnosed herself as a "highly sensitive person."

The community pool was the closest I got to transcendence.

While Rush worked out—even the mechanics of gym equipment overwhelm me—I sat on the sidelines and silently cheered the girls on.

Oldest scissored her legs sideways through the water as if she could will herself to swim with effort alone. *You're already enough*, I told her with a feeble thumbs-up.

Youngest waited and listened and watched before launching off from the edge with body strong. *Trust yourself, little one*, I declared with a mimed clap.

Middle bounced happily in the shallows until she had to put her whole raven-haired head under water and came up a blubber of snot and tears. *You're more capable than you know,* I promised, holding her in the force field of my sight.

Wordlessly, weightlessly, I celebrated every small stroke that had nothing to do with me.

It was indeed a strange comfort that the girls and their abilities had nothing to do with me, not genetically at least. Biological parents often talked about the charm of seeing themselves in their children. "She's an exact replica, humor and everything," a proud friend marveled while I drank kombucha and nodded without knowing.

It's not like I never imagined the possibility. I imagined she would be a city person, a wanderer with fine hair and freckled legs who was never stumped by a sidewalk's end. I imagined he'd be a conversationalist, a word nerd, alphabet soup for a brain, and a studious, receding chin. What would that feel like to talk with, to walk with?

I didn't know.

I didn't need to.

Because not seeing your kids as fun-sized versions of yourself had its appeal, too.

Once, at a public lecture, I was confiding to a colleague how hereditary nonattachment felt like one of the unsung joys of fostering, when a woman sitting in front of us turned around. "It really is the best," she whispered, as if discussing a secret route to buried treasure. "I love watching my adopted son be terrible at things I'm great at and great at things I'm terrible at."

Now, really, every child is an amalgamation of old and new, inheritance and chance, someone's person and her own person, but nonbiological parenting sure helps you hold the mystery lightly. It helps you hold your ego lightly, too, and there is a soft mischief in this. From the beginning, whether my family would sink or swim depended on so much more than Rush and me. It depended on a whole ecology of other adults.

Foster parenting was by definition shared parenting, a team sport in which individual achievements were far less important than the success of the whole. In most cases, our coaches emphasized that reunification, not adoption, was the goal. Still, our classmates in training asked, "How often do we have to meet with the social worker?" and "What's the fastest you've seen the termination of parental rights happen?"

I got the feeling that fostering was, for some, like a gestational green room before the real work of parenting began. All the intrusions into their homes and schedules and lifestyle choices could be tolerated until that hoped-for day came when they could raise their children, like other self-reliant Americans, in private. But parenting in private sounded awful to me.

While I bristled at small, frequent, *assaultive* interruptions to my work life, I lived for interruptions to my child-rearing life. Neediness, it turns out, is a wonderful aphrodisiac for community. Every appointment on our calendar was another chance to check in with another adult and ask, "What would you do? And am I doing it okay?"

There was the girls' social worker who invited us to regularly frame each child's development as a series of strengths and needs. (Strength: healthy appetite. Need: vegetable variety.) A guardian ad litem patiently answered all our dense and repetitive questions about the court proceedings. Oldest started seeing a therapeutic social worker who specialized in childhood trauma. There was even a social worker who met with us every three months to see how our marriage was faring.

And it was all paid for. Even the swim lessons.

I remarked to a friend, "If this kind of government support came built-in for biological parents, how many fewer foster parents would we need?"

Sometimes the girls and I would arrive at the pool early enough to see the toddler class finishing up. The four of us would sit on the bleachers staring at each parent with the buoyant eyes and each child with the sagging diaper. From where I sat, the little ones exhibited none of the stiff-neck effort, self-conscious caution, or terror of trying I saw in our three girls. Maybe it would come. Surely it would come, right? For now, the pairs were locked only on each other.

It was in those moments that a quiet envy I could not speak slid down my throat. At the risk of deluding myself, I was not, I don't think, envious of the parents who the toddlers reached for with their balloon-animal arms. I was envious of the toddlers who, in comparison to my girls, were growing up with an attachment both singular and sure.

I was also annoyed that, despite my aggressive delight in unlikely families, traditional ones seemed so much easier.

The Myth of Traditional Families

It is autumn now, and I am going through old letters, old pictures, old files. A postcard from my older brother, Charlie, ends up on top of the pile, stamped "Mailed by Mule" at the bottom of the Grand Canyon. "Typical," I shake my head. Always adventuring. Making home wherever, with whomever, he goes. Though maybe I'm trying to do the same, just without all the breathtaking views.

When I was smaller, in both size and mind, I likely defined the "traditional" family as the one Charlie and I inherited— married man and woman mixed to yield two parts biological boy and girl. This was, I thought, the recipe for the American Dream. The Gold Standard. The Christian Ideal.

Our parents' divorce eventually saved me from that brand of righteousness but prompted another. I set off to redeem as asset what the world called deficit: the *broken* family, the *blended* family, the *alternative* family. "For the wisdom of this world is foolishness," read the words in my Teen Life Bible, and I believed them. I needed to believe them, my solace and armor.

The Bible, as it turns out, is a terrific text if ever you need evidence of your traditional family's fallibility. The first book alone is downright Shakespearean in plot. Barren wife forces female slave to sleep with aging husband. Mother helps younger son deceive father for the family blessing. Sister becomes jealous of sister's fertility and, in a fury fit for a stage, screams at shared husband, "Give me children—or I will die!" And these don't even account for some of the more horrific crimes committed by badly behaving kinfolk. My own family's crimes looked like a daytime soap opera by comparison.

So, while the Bible paints a vivid picture of traditional families, it's not the picture most Americans seek to emulate. If it were, forced surrogacy might still be a fine way to start a family, family blessings might still be reserved for firstborn sons (daughters might still largely be considered property), and polygamy, as in the case of the aforementioned sister wives, might still be common practice.

Instead, it's the nuclear family that has become synonymous with the traditional family in the United States, even though it's been well-documented that such a family form didn't even exist until the last century—and faded just as soon as it soared. How this image of family—biological, conjugal, and of a manageable size—is so popular among Christians baffles me, given that Jesus appears belligerently uninterested in (and, obviously, categorically unaware of) it.

Over and over as I pored through the translucent pages of my neon-blue Bible, I noticed Jesus refusing to identify with his traditional family and instead spinning a new vision of family: one in which shared practice, not shared parentage, binds together the people of God. A family that is more made than begotten. A family in which there is no mine or yours.

After all, the text said, God can create kinship out of anyone, out of anything, even stones.*

It's SARAH WHO tells me how Mother Earth does roughly the same thing.

Sarah is a forty-six-year-old foster parent who lives in the Idaho River Valley. Our lives intersected moons ago after I read her memoir about loving and leaving Christianity. (When I ask her if she left because of its hostility to biologically childless women like herself, she says, "I never felt victimized as a woman who wasn't a mother in Christianity. I just felt victimized as a woman.") Now she's written a

---

* This sentiment, one of my favorites in all the scriptures, comes courtesy of Jesus's locust-and-honey-eating cousin John. Speaking to his followers, he chides, "Do not begin to say to yourselves, 'We have Abraham as our ancestor'; for I tell you, God is able from these stones to raise up children to Abraham" (Luke 3:8). With his trademark lack of tact, John is telling them that it doesn't matter whether the family line is blood or not, legitimate or not, natural or not, when God has always been about the miracle of a bigger—*supra*natural—belonging.

book called *Stranger Care* about our ability to care for those who don't come assigned to us. The trees are good at this, she says.

Sarah explains, "I was interested intellectually with this idea of kinship, that there are things that are related that we don't think of as related." Even over the phone, I can hear the pace of her voice propel. "Like, how am I related to that tree? How is that tree related to that bee? You know, how do we depend on each other in these radical ways? What would it look like to attend to one another as family?"

To be sure, attending to the trees and bees as family was not the original reason why I opted to be childfree. I count it one of the great failures of my formation that I know little about Mother Earth, but I have been reading more about her and her kind of non-blood love. At night, when the light is low and the dog sleeps stiff, I have been learning about the council of pecan trees from Robin Wall Kimmerer's *Braiding Sweetgrass*.

Pecans, Kimmerer writes, are peculiar trees. They don't crop every year. Instead, they scan their environment to gauge the needs of the season. Squirrels too fat? Better hold back. Only a few hawks left? Time to go nuts. (Forgive me.) Even in times of plenty, though, the nuts are meant to be gathered and stored, their protective hard shell both a warning and an urging: Go slow, be wise, wait awhile.

Did you know pecans are a kind of fruit, too? Their rallying cry: "Be fruitful and fortify."

But it's not just that pecan trees are known for being leathery or discerning that endears me to them. It's that they move collectively. Kimmerer explains the majesty of their mast (*mast* meaning synchronous) fruiting process:

> If one tree fruits, they all fruit—there are no soloists. Not one tree in a grove, but the whole grove; not one grove in the forest, but every grove; all across the country and all across the state. The trees act not as individuals, but somehow as a collective. Exactly how they do this, we don't yet know. But what we see is the power of unity. What happens to one happens to us all. We can starve together or feast together. All flourishing is mutual.[2]

Put this way, the pecan trees sound a lot like other women I've talked to who've scanned the world we live in— temperature spikes and racial violence, mass shootings and ocean surges—and decided it's not the time for a new crop of children. There is enough burden on Mother Earth. Our reproductive choices are a way to mother her in return.

Indeed, for all our talk of "going green" through recycling or becoming vegan or embracing walkability (my girls, at the moment, are militant about metal straws), none of these "personal lifestyle choices" come close to reducing greenhouse gas emissions like having one fewer child than planned does in developed countries. So, why is this way of bearing fruit any less faithful than traditional parenting?

I ask Sarah if environmental reasons prompted her to embrace an alternative family of her own. Not exactly, she says. It was more like supporting evidence for a deeper awareness. In her book, she describes how she longed to become a mother, imagined she'd become a mother, had picked out names and pictured her pregnancy. It was her husband who worried about adding another child to the planet. So, deadlocked, the two went to therapy, then just Sarah went to therapy, then gradually the question in her head blinked from *Do I want to have a baby?* to *Do I want to be a parent?* The idea to foster-to-adopt offered a middle ground between biological parenting and not parenting at all.

"And then as soon as we started, as soon as we became foster parents, when we brought our foster daughter home, I mean the connection was immediate," Sarah tells me. She had heard biological parents talk about that moment in the birthing room when their capacity to experience a great big love birthed, too. Honestly? It had always irritated her as a person without kids. Who were they to imply what she was or wasn't capable of experiencing?

But now it was all so obvious to her: Family had nothing to do with blood, and everything to do with choice. "I think there's this fundamental misunderstanding," she says. "We feel our hearts expand, maybe, when we have a biological kid, and we confuse that expansion with biology. But, really, it's about what we choose to tend."

I think again about the dwindling hawks and the potbellied squirrels and the pecan trees, tending the earth in their measured, sometimes barren, way. Maybe we can't change the kind of tree we are—I do not come from a line of an unwavering evergreens—but we can look to the trees for the kind of beings we are: wildly connected and radically dependent on each other.

Before we hang up, Sarah offers her own warning and urging: "We tell these stories about what counts as family and who counts as kin that limit our own capacities. But I think, as humans, we're much more capable of love than we admit."

I WANT TO believe Sarah.

But given my familial history, given my theological inheritance, I worry I've been shaped to put too much faith in the elasticity of family. After all, once you make it past the dramatic opening acts of the Bible, it's not the traditional family but the adopted family that's prized as the model for humanity. The adopted family, you might say, is the real Christian Ideal. The true Gold Standard. Not the American Dream but God's.

It's true that after the arrival of Jesus on the scene, some Christians saw the household not as an extension of the biological family but a replacement for it: "an itinerant group of men and women unrelated to one another by blood or marriage, most of whom had also apparently separated from their families."[3] A longing for spiritual brothers and sisters was ultimately meant to supplant the need for biological ones. The ideal family was not stable, small, natural. It was fluid, inclusive, improbable.

Which must be where all my optimism about fostering came from.

"It'll be different with your own," well-meaning parents used to assure Rush and me when we were still childfree. It was normal not to like other people's children, they consoled. But everyone loved their own children, *everyone*. It was an assumption few challenged: You will never love a shared child as much as your blood child.

I remember thinking these comments strange coming from people who called themselves church family. What do you mean? I wanted to ask. Isn't that what we're here for? To love those we have no earthly reason to love? To love who God loves?

But I had not yet accounted for the slimy feeling of envy at the pool. The arrival of that feeling, a few short months into fostering, threatened to undermine decades of my best and most beautiful defenses.

Family Visits

In the picture, Youngest frowns. She is still six years old. Her eyes are blank. On her body hangs a denim top with tulle bottom that appears four sizes too big. If she didn't look so sad, I might laugh. It nearly swallows her, both the garment and the grief.

Once a month, while in foster care, the girls had supervised time with their birth family. On those days, their social worker picked them up early from school and drove them to the Department of Social Services, where they spent two hours visiting with their relatives in a room that resembled an efficiency apartment minus the bed. They lived for those two hours. The comfort of their favorite foods. The unspoken language of screens. Plastic bags full of clothes.

You can believe in shared parenting and still loathe its aftermath.

The girls returned home after every visit grumpier than the day before. And they had every right to be. And it was ruinous. It was ruinous because Rush would be making a dinner that no one was hungry for, and I would be making small talk that no one was interested in, and the girls wouldn't be making out very well at all. They whined. They interrupted. They came home with new clothes but no new closet space.

Our first Child and Family Team meeting took place in June. Child and Family Team meetings or CFTs—everything in government work was condensed to the benignancy of abbreviations—are a time to discuss the permanency plan. It is not unusual for there to be more than one plan. The thinking went that if and when reunification was no longer the plan, then a plan for adoption could be more swiftly implemented.

Best laid plans aside, the CFT meetings were also a rare opportunity to speak directly to the birth parents, if involved, and for this I was relieved. To our first meeting, I brought a new list of questions, different than the groundless ones asked in January. How did you care for the girls when they were sick? What vegetables have they tried, and how were they cooked? I read from a script that I'd written nervously in drippy, black ink: *Thank you for the clothes. You know them well. Please do not send more.*

While waiting for the request to take effect, we had started a one-in, one-out rule. For every piece of clothing that came into the house, a quick check: Do you like it? Does it fit? Is it in decent shape, like "yes" to a few stains but "no" to shoes with the soles coming unglued? If every answer was affirmative, she could keep it, but it would cost her one like item. A shirt for a shirt. A skort for a skort. A fake-fur hoodie for a cheetah-print head wrap? I'll allow it.

The one-in, one-out rule was a crushing blow to their little maximalist hearts. They didn't want to get rid of anything. "Offer to take a picture of them wearing whatever they give away," a social worker counseled. "Tell them they can look at it whenever they want. They'll likely never ask." We did. And they didn't. Every single time, the anticipation of letting go was more terrible than the thing itself. Looking at the picture of Youngest now, I want to tell her, "Oh, honey. The loss never changes, but you do."

We were seven months into fostering when I realized I hadn't purchased more than a bag of socks for the girls. After sharing this bit of information with a friend, she asked flatly, "Would you like to be able to pick out clothes for them?" A flush flirted with my cheeks. My eyes rounded like two tiny moons. I'd become so skilled at nonattachment that the idea of attachment—what would that even involve?—felt like another galaxy, a billion bright and hazy miles away.

The Myth of Chosen Families

I pull out the foster training manual from a felt file box in my closet. It's right there—Meeting 1, Handout 2, Page 2, "Criteria for Mutual Selection of Foster and Adoptive Parents," #6: Be loss and attachment experts. I couldn't say they didn't warn me; only that I felt more prepared for the first than the second. So, I set out to catch up.

Attachment theory was first developed in the 1940s by an upper-crust English psychoanalyst named John Bowlby who claimed that a child's behavior was a result of their earliest relationships. And there was no relationship more pivotal, he believed, than that of the birth mother. Her skin, her gaze, her voice, her ability to respond to her child's needs was the ground in which a life of security grew. A securely attached child was poised to become a productive member of society while an insecurely attached child was prone to anxiety, depression, delinquency, neurosis, and the development of "an affectionless psychopathic character."[4]

What a marvelous privilege and pressure for a woman to bear.

The good news is that secure attachments prove to be the norm around the world. It's evolutionary, after all, thought Bowlby, for a child to bond with their primary caregiver. Any number of caregivers could conceivably meet the needs of a child, but Bowlby proposed that children were motivated to choose one in particular with whom to develop their fundamental patterns of belonging. If not the birth mother, then "a permanent mother substitute—one person who steadily 'mothers'"—could do, but there was not much time for the doing.[5] The critical window of attachment was six months through about age two and a half—at most.

In this light, the earnest questions in foster training about, "How young do they come?" made some sense. Rush and I had traded the critical window of attachment to meet the critical needs of older children—and our own, too, for equal partnership and a good night's sleep. When I ask Rush now what he loves best about nonbiological parenting, he enthuses, "Oh, definitely skipping the first five years. We were not cut out for that crap."

That crap, however, is something special. John Bowlby's work was something special, too, for demonstrating how our bodies depend on one another for more than a meal—we need a map. We need someone else to corroborate our map of the world and where we belong in it. Not the fantasy of belonging. But the mundanity of it. The way something as small as our breath tells her, "It's safe to stay awhile." Or how a soft hand on a bony shoulder says to him, "This is hard, and you are held." Those stupid, darling voices we do that mean, "God, I like you." Attachment theory was revolutionary for the enormous worth it put in intimate gestures to claim someone as your *own*.

It was not revolutionary for assuming that those gestures were best when modeled by a mother.

Since the invention of attachment theory, scientists have found that, yes, our birth mother matters but, no, she is not the only or even our brightest hope for belonging. This is not a revelation to the many communities of color who, whether out of need or insight, have long practiced the magic of shared care. "The reality is, black families are expansive, fluid, and brilliantly rely on the support, knowledge, and capacity of 'the village' to take care of each other," says family activist Mia Birdsong.[6] Neuroscientist Bruce Perry argues that it's that kind of relational diversity our bodies crave, calling the hyperfocus on the nuclear family "disrespectful of the brain's potential."[7]

Still, a slithering question I cannot shake remains. What chance is there for the extended or chosen family if the first family failed—and failed for a very long time—to supply the nutrients a child needed? If attachment is like the soil of caregiving, would loving someone with attachment "issues" always be, as one social worker described it, like pouring water onto an impenetrable earth? The effort sounded awfully demoralizing.

You understand then that I am not coming to this research unbiased.

JOHN BOWLBY WAS right that every human being needs at least one person to call *my* person. But there's nothing in the research that says we can't call on more. It's true that our early attachments irrevocably change the way our body reads the map of the world and our place in it. It's also true that early trauma can be "patched" by people who don't come assigned to us.

So, although we may never be able to erase trauma's effects, we can help others flex their capacities through things like yoga or therapy, storytelling or theater. We can see trauma's symptoms as part of someone's superpower—all the strategies their body has tried to help them to survive. We can take a break from studying the soil for a while and realize that the seed is a sight to behold, too.

It occurs to me now that much of attachment theory is from the perspective of a child and how a child moves toward her caregiver. But what about the rest of us, I wonder? What about how a parent chooses a child who doesn't come assigned to them? Or, likewise, how a friend chooses a friend? In their book, *Big Friendship*, Aminatou Sow and Ann Friedman highlight research that suggests a well-attached friendship—in which there's mutual delight, a secure base of belonging, and a safe harbor for support—is a lot like a well-attached family.[8] It makes sense, then, that these kinds of friendships are sometimes called *chosen family*.

Chosen family is a popular term among young people these days, although the notion was birthed decades ago. There is a beautiful confidence to this phrase that I will never stop loving, perhaps most of all for its ability to repair the absence of agency many of us felt in our first families. (Did you know developing a sense of agency is a balm for healing trauma?) But maybe it's because I've started to feel a little less young— weirdly, even my eyes are going gray—that I've started to worry about the weight of choice. A family built on choice alone implies it can be unchosen. We don't talk about that.

The language of choice is used *carefully* in the foster and adopting world for this reason: If a child thinks she is chosen, then she might work to remain so, trying to earn by effort what is supposedly unconditional by birth. Few biological parents, it's assumed, would consider calling the government if their child proved harder to love than hoped.

Contrast that assumption with an activity Rush and I did in our foster parent training in which we were encouraged to list any deal-breaking behaviors. (You remember: the poop throwing, back talking, dog kicking.) This activity was one of the things that reassured me most about our decision to foster. It acknowledged the limits of human love when the rest of the world kept on insisting—and guilting us for feeling—otherwise.

For a lot of people, I suppose, fostering and adoption is supposed to prove the opposite: It's supposed to prove that anyone can become your own if you choose. For this reason adoption's been called "a quintessentially American institution" because it epitomizes "the recklessly optimistic faith in self-construction and social engineering that characterizes much of our history."[9] But this kind of thinking has proven to have its own limits. The discriminatory practices against adopters. The fetishization of "exotic" adoptees. Sometimes, even now, our transracial family feels like it warrants an apology: I'm sorry for the disruption of your culture. I wish it'd turned out differently for your community. I promise I didn't choose this, not exactly.

I'm sorry I studied French.

SARAH HAD SAID we love those whom we choose to tend.

Her words remind me of a quotation I keep coming across in the handful of parenting books I have allowed myself to read. "It's not so much that we care for children because we love them, as that we love them because we care for them," writes child psychologist Alison Gopnik in *The Philosophical Baby*.[10] Everyone loves this quotation. Ezra Klein loves this quotation. Goodness, I love this quotation.

But after sitting with it some more, rolling it around on my tongue, spitting it out in conversation, I've been wondering if it was really intended for me, decidedly not the parent of three philosophical babies but three older, guarded girls. What if choice alone is not enough to bind someone to you, to bind you to them?

Holding the heft of the foster training binder in my hands, I'm starting to think that choice is only part of the story. I'm starting to think that to choose someone as your own, you have to feel yourselves claimed by something greater than human love alone. Call it God. Call it chemistry. Call it ecology.

Sarah had called it the universe. I nearly missed this part of her story. But going back through my notes from our conversation, it's there, this feeling of otherworldly assignment to love and know and grow her foster daughter. "I kind of felt the universe saying, like here, tend, tend this, tend her," she said.

So, truly, call it whatever you want, but I'm starting to think you have to feel yourself worthy of love and assigned by love to the people you call family. I'm convinced this is what protects us from choosing only people who are easy to love. I'm convinced this is the only thing that makes choosing people we have no business choosing possible.

There's no denying that some loves do flow more naturally. I think again of the trees. After a little more digging, I discover that many trees do take care of their "own" first. They can recognize their kin and send nutrients to their kin and give information to their kin that helps the family line survive. But they also help other species when it's good for the whole. It's not exactly like they "choose" this fate. It's just what they do. It's who they are. It's who we are. *All flourishing is mutual.*

So, will it be different with your own?

Depending on the day, I can argue both ways.

To the parents who say of fostering or adopting, "I could never do what you do," I want to say you already are. Every parent is an uncertainty specialist. No parent knows their place in perpetuity. Relinquishing love is the work of us all.

And yet there are also days when I want to say, "No, Normals, raising a child who has lost family before you ever become family is not the same.

"There are times you want to scream the sadness right out of them and there are times you want to reach across the room for them, if they would let you, but you're not sure they'd let you, because you're not sure they like you, and living with people who don't like you, or, at least, wish they'd had no reason to meet you, is a terrible pain to bear but you bear it because you can. You can bear the sadness, yours and theirs.

"This is a surprise to you, and when you are on the elliptical, but only when you are elliptical, you nearly shimmer with sweat thinking about how this surprise sometimes feels a lot like happy."

So, it's different, and it isn't.

A better question, I've decided, is: Who is my own?

Moments

July 11, 2016

Dear Friends,

An update, this one in moments.

Moment: I get an e-mail, shortly after our first Child and Family Team meeting in June, that says the Department of Social Services is redoubling their efforts for birth family reunification. Relief floods my tired, tired body. We have been praying for this outcome, when we remember to pray at all.

Moment: I am at a friend's pool with the girls. Where once my sitting on the sidelines had been a show of support, now it is insulting. "Erin, when are you getting in the water?" they ask on the hour, every hour. I give them the nonanswer that has become my standard, "Soon, maybe."

Moment: Another e-mail, this one in July, from the social worker. The termination of parental rights has already been filed. What happened to redoubling efforts? We're full steam on adoption. Driving home on the freeway with the wind so loud it drowns out my weaker voices, I hear myself say, "Here I am."

Moment: Over a watery gin and tonic, I wonder aloud to another mother how I might better show up at church. (I am always wondering.) She says maybe my greatest witness to this church is showing up with my blended family every week. "How lovely," I think, and "Screw you, too." This is hard for a woman to hear.

Moment: It's nighttime. I'm leaving the girls' bedroom when I hear Oldest toss a casual "Love you" my way. I told myself I wouldn't say it unless one of them said it, and now one has, so I say, "Love you, too" before closing the door. I nosedive onto my bed like a schoolgirl, drowning in a pool of vulnerability.

So be it,

Erin

MOVEMENT III

Savoring a Life
Well-Lived

CHAPTER 7

Script: You'll Regret Not Having Kids

Rewrite: Kids Are Not an Insurance Policy

There is a time in our lives, usually in mid-life, when a woman has to make a decision—possibly the most important psychic decision of her future life—and that is, whether to be bitter or not.

—CLARISSA PINKOLA ESTÉS[1]

NOW THAT I have sat at the feet of revolutionary mothers like Jessica, now that I have embraced my good pleasure with Karen and Melody, now that I have accepted (or reaccepted) my assignment to tend with Sarah, I have decided to try and reckon with it. The "it" part is becoming clearer. It is not mothering as an act of caregiving but motherhood as an institution—an exclusive, sanctified, narrowly human institution—I object to. I get to work preparing fifty pages of a new manuscript that is big enough to include the childfree, the childfull, and me.

Not unrelated, I also start reading a lot of poetry.

———

I FELL IN love with poetry late in life, and by late in life, I mean my late twenties.

Graduate school had finished with all the fanfare of a driveway fireworks show. Now what? No easy answers in sight, I kept writing, found a freelance gig doing book publicity, and because neither of those paid enough to support regular haircuts, applied to become a vocational retreat facilitator helping people discern the most important decisions of their lives. Poetry is useful for this kind of discernment, though the whole point of poetry is to be less concerned with usefulness and more concerned with loveliness. Loving loveliness is still new to me.

At the Quaker nonprofit where I trained and worked, we used poetry as a reflection tool. But it was also more than a reflection tool; it was an escape hatch out of the hegemony of our big, sensible brains. So, the point wasn't to flex our literary skills. (Thank God, given the only English credit I took in college was a film course.) The point was to consider our lives in a different light, out of the direct heat of prose where *it must be decided one way or the other* and into the soft glow of a poem where *well, yes, now, both could be true*.

A retreat went something like this. Participants would come for a day, the weekend, a series of weekends, to sit in a circle and attend to their inner teacher. Attending to the inner teacher is simply a Quaker way of saying *checking in with your center, tuning in to your true self,* or *listening for the holy within.* (It is like a fierce inventory in this way.) This is a practice, of course, that anyone can do from anywhere, but it helps to have some other pathfinders walking the labyrinth of your life with you. It also helps to have no Wi-Fi and paper handouts.

Imagine you receive a handout in such a circle. (You'll forgive the facilitator who got creative with the sponge-paint-looking card stock.) You came to this retreat because you are at a juncture in the road or knee-deep in the weeds. Clarity is what you're after, even though the facilitator has told you repeatedly that faithfulness is today's goal. Faithfulness sounds a whole lot like an organizational ass-covering measure to you, but you are nevertheless determined to get the most out of your time here.

So, you train your gaze toward the text on your lap. "Now I become myself. It's taken / Time, many years and places."[2] The poem is by May Sarton. It's not one you've seen before. The facilitator reads it aloud. She has come up with a series of questions to aid your reflection, printed neatly on a nearby flip chart. "What has been dissolved and shaken in you? When have you felt the pieces of who you are falling into place? What do you want to celebrate about who you are becoming now?"

You roll your eyes at first. You feel an inexplicable urge to go to the bathroom. Then, slowly, if you can stand the whirr of your own brain, there is the sound of a thought being tied off like a balloon. Then another. By the time the facilitator asks you to find a partner with whom you can share a revelation or two, you're hanging on to a small bundle of somethings that can take you somewhere. It's encouraging, and only a little embarrassing.

The poetry, the reflecting, the sharing, it's all meant to lead to the mountaintop of discernment, or something called a Clearness Committee. A Clearness Committee is simply a smaller group of people, with some pretty important ground rules, who gather to help someone sort themselves out. But it's how someone gets sorted that's the real magic of the method. And it's not by getting some sage advice. Or an expert book recommendation. Though I do covet both in other contexts.

Instead, insight comes from being listened to, really listened to, for two, whole, human hours. One person has the floor. The other three or four are witnesses, wayfinders, there only to refine knowings rather than to enforce them. There is often more poetry to ground the time, storytelling and silence, questions and mirroring, and at the end, the most remarkable feeling of being alone, together. *Nobody can live this life for me,* you think, and *Nobody expects me to go it alone.*

If you can believe it—which of course you can by now—this is the process by which I decided to become a parent, permanently. How do you decide, if it is a decision at all? (You already know. It is frequently not.) A friend who mothers two feral boys concedes, "It's not like you can try them out first!"

to which I say, "Aha! But this is not so!" Isn't that exactly what Rush and I did by fostering? We tested out a life we could not imagine otherwise.

My question now is: Did it matter? How much data did we really have when we set out? How much data does one really need? How does anyone know what will be good for the *us* we have yet to become? Is there any defense against regret in the end? And if there are regrets, what is the salve? What makes the difference between regretting a life and savoring a life?

And can this remedy soothe me, by which I mean, is it truly useful?

The Threat of Regret

Back when people used to stand in line at their local bank, Rush and I waited patiently between the velvet ropes at ours.

We were just married, twenty-four and twenty-two respectively, which was younger than the national average of first nuptials in our day but older than the national average during our grandparents'. So, old enough. Old enough to be standing in a line at a local bank, clutching a physical checkbook.

It was while standing in line that an older man from town—somewhere between our age and our grandparents'—approached us with the bald confidence of a Southerner.

"Married now?" He nodded at Rush. Rush nodded back. I hid a grimace.

It never went well, in my experience, talking to strangers about marriage or motherhood. Too much baggage. Too little time to unpack. Indecent to do so publicly. Like watching a TSA agent rifle through your one-size-fits-most thongs.

"I don't suppose it'll be long now before you've got little rascals running 'round!" the man continued, chest puffed.

No longer able to resist, I put my rigid body in front of his and piped in, "Actually, we're not planning on having any."

Undaunted, he brushed my nonsense away as if I were a gnat, irritating but ultimately insignificant. "You may feel that way now, but you'll change your mind. You'll see."

All I could see at the moment was a way out of the conversation. The teller waved us forward, like we were boats on a sloppy sea and she a flag from friendly territory.

I WISH I could report that this conversation was a fluke. A memorable but harmless anecdote about the perils of small-town small talk. But too many women have shared similar tales. The message goes something like this: Everybody has kids. Or regrets not having kids. You don't want regrets. You'll change your mind.

It's a dumb premise. But it's a bulwark one as far as premises go, rooted in a patriarchal worldview in which thoughts are supposed to stack up linearly, stability is damn close to divinity, and changing your mind is the worst fate imaginable. It's also a decidedly feminine fate. Circular thinking is a sign of confusion, or women who can't get to the point fast enough. Flexibility is labeled flighty, or women who can't stay in one place long enough. "You'll change your mind" is both a paternalistic pat on the back and a warning to nonconforming women; fall into line or face the threat of regret.

Regret, I've gathered, is also a bitch.

Threat of regret is a powerful motivator of human behavior. It's why we sometimes RSVP "yes" to the party, to the conference, to the girls' trip, not because we want to but because it'd feel worse not to. We're afraid of missing out. We're afraid of being forgotten. It's why we sometimes commit to more projects than we can complete in a season. We're worried about the opportunities drying up if we don't. We're worried about being worried in the future. Threat of regret may even be why some people become parents, trusting that today's risk will yield tomorrow's dividends. "Children are no longer economic assets," author Jennifer Senior writes, "so the only way to balance the books is to assume they are *future* assets, which requires an awful lot of investment, not to mention faith."[3]

This faith isn't exactly wrong.

At least, not according to the dark hole of psychology journals I've fallen into recently. While the research on regret paints a layered picture—for instance, there's no easy answer to what makes us sorrier, failures of action or inaction—studies have found that "the extent to which a regretted decision constitutes a threat to the individual's sense of belonging" (not attending the party, not taking on the project, not having the children) "has an important influence on the intensity of regret felt."[4]

Which explains why the threat of regret is a strategy used by parents to convince nonparents and even not-so-prolific parents to conform. (The perceived "normative parameters" of parents are minuscule—between two and three but not more than four children.) Not only is conformity socially satisfying but it's also personally validating of the majority's life trajectory. This many people could not be wrong about this one thing, we think, and if they are, at least we will be wrong together. Parenting in a pack is surer, safer, a defense against becoming plucked off, one by one, by our rapacious doubts.

And so, childless women—ideally older, mournful childless women—become object lessons.

I'M THINKING NOW of a story Margaret shared with me.

Margaret is the daughter of an African Methodist Episcopal pastor and a school counselor. When she was little, she proudly declared to her parents, "I'm never getting married. I'm never having kids." Her mom, who'd been raised in a large family, didn't understand and told her so. Her dad had subtler strategies for steering her back on course, not unlike those of President Roosevelt who long ago thought a study in contrasts could rouse the childless to join ranks.

In high school, Margaret's dad invited her to tag along on

a pastoral visit. She reflects, "He took me with him to this woman's house who he was serving communion to. And she was older, single, *lonely*. That's how he described her: this *lonely* old woman who lives by herself. She doesn't have any children; she's never been married. So, he takes me to her house. We sat in the house, talked, had a good time. She laughed." I love that Margaret remembers her laughing.

Margaret continues, "And then he said when we left, 'You see how lonely she is?' And I said, 'Dad, she doesn't look lonely to me!'" Now it's Margaret's turn to laugh. "And then he said, 'Well, that's because we came to visit her!' And I said, 'She looks pretty happy to me.' And he said, 'But why do you want to be alone? Like, not have anyone?' And I said, 'Dad, some people are happier that way.'"

Margaret's young intuition was right. Not *everyone* is happier to grow old without the socially condoned comfort of children, but many researchers have found no special suffering among childless women late in life—not socially, not financially, not psychologically. Women who are intentionally childless have even reported becoming *more* comfortable and confident in their choices over time. But it's not just the child-free who experience an increase in mental health as they age. In one study I find, women as a whole reported reaching their peak happiness after age eighty-five, presumably when they have the least caregiving responsibilities of their adult lives.[5] When I tell my girls this, they do not believe me; Oldest says, "I think your twenties are your prime."

But it's quite the opposite for the childless.

If looking for an object lesson in loneliness, we'd be better off pointing to younger people, people in their early forties, late thirties, even, yes, their twenties. (It's hard not to recall the "ministry of availability" and the earnest, epic failure that was.) This is when social isolation *actually* peaks among people without children, according to sociologist Eric Klinenberg, and it's not because they're sitting around eating potato chips and stroking their cats and pining for a life they don't have.[6] So, what is the culprit? The mass retreat of peers into the domestic sphere.

Janell offers an illustration. "I had a conversation a few weeks ago; I wasn't bemoaning. I may have been complaining. I felt like I was just naming a sort of loss or a sadness in wanting to have time with a particular friend who was in the throes of early mothering, when an older woman looked at me knowingly and said, 'You just have to let them be *enslaved* to their children for those first few years. They'll come back.'"

Janell's chin recedes into her neck, her eyeballs huge. "And I thought, number one, I'm uncomfortable with your use of that word in this context, and number two, like, really? It felt like a denial of my sadness for the lack of availability or lack of presence or even like lack of basic eye contact from this specific friend in this season."

Even so, Janell's interlocutor was somewhat right in her reassurance. According to the research, "older parents are as likely to sustain close friendships as older nonparents."[7] But for a while, at least, Klinenberg says, watching friends sustain their own families instead is the biggest stress point for the childless—more than the fear of aging or dying alone.

So, if not childlessness, what does make elderly women especially depressed? Two things: poor health and poverty, neither of which is automatically eased by the existence of available children or adorable grandchildren. In fact, according to one book I pick up, "motherhood is the single biggest risk factor for poverty in old age."[8]

The statistics subvert the assumptions, don't they? Parenthood, not childlessness, is thought to be the insurance policy against future misery. *Who will take care of you when you're older?* our peers may wonder. *What will we talk about if not our grandkids?* our own parents may worry. It's not just the young who crave safety in groups. Children are like conversational guardrails, familiar, sturdy.

Still, if friends and family truly are anxious about our well-being (or theirs), you might tell them that Social Security, Medicare, and Medicaid all turn out to be better protectives against misery in old age than one's kids.

Perhaps now would be a good time to mention that not one of the women I talked to was opposed to other people speaking genuinely about their own experiences, though preferably without a velvet rope in between them.

Em, thirty-four and divorced, gets the impulse of friends to proselytize even as she is practicing speaking her truth with tact. "A few weeks ago, my friend asked me, 'Do you ever think about being a single mom? Like, you could do it. You could.' I felt too bad to shut her down. And so, what came out of my mouth was, 'Well, if I had a husband . . .' or 'I'm already older . . .'" Em admits. "But I should have just said, 'No, that's not my calling in my life.'"

Em's calling in life, if anyone is paying attention, is spectacularly clear. She runs a successful boutique and coworking space in downtown Raleigh, a million-dollar business with the goal of encouraging women to use their influence for good. So, it's not like she's barren of achievement. But even as we're sitting cross-legged in my living room, she reads a text thread in which one of her friends is being praised as a "badass" for pumping breast milk in the bathroom of a music venue. "I can't tell you the last time they told me I was badass for running my own business."

"So, I know my friend wants me to be happy," Em says, returning to her original thought. "She wants me to be full of joy. She's experiencing joy through motherhood, and that's what she wants me to experience, too," Em reasons. "And so, I don't hate her. I'm not mad. I'm more angry at this cultural narrative."

THERE'S NOT A lot of sympathy for regret in the American narrative. Regret is weak, whiny, pitiful, not positive, not productive, not empowering, unfeminist even. So, it's natural that we'd try to protect each other from it. But however well-intentioned the "you'll change your mind" line may be, there is simply not enough evidence to support the claim.

Besides, I want to know, why can't a change of mind be a mark of maturity?

Take Margaret's dad. He changed his mind over time. He's come to accept that motherhood is not Margaret's future. "Now he's shifted a lot of his thoughts toward making sure that I have close relationships with family," Margaret says. She imagines one of her nephews will end up taking care of her when she's older. (From where I'm sitting, she's also nurtured a network of grown women who'd do the same.) "So, you know, [my dad's] just making sure I'm tethered."

Tethered. I can grab on to this word, feel it in my hands like a rope with heft, a rope that burns. We should be so lucky to be tethered to two or three people who will tell us the truth about life, theirs and ours. You could say that the Clearness Committee was an invitation for a few friends to hold that line with us. We weren't looking for definitive answers, although those are always nice. We were just looking for a life we could live with and people to live it with, which, looking back now, seems like asking for a lot and very little all at once.

The Questions Are Your Answer

A bald-headed priest greeted us.

Rush and I had arrived at the mid-century ranch house after a short drive through the North Carolina suburbs and into the yawning, green countryside. I can't exactly remember what the interior of the house looked like, only that it was *homey*, a mishmash of flooring, lumpy couches, lamps with tipsy shades. In any case, it wasn't an actual house that actual people lived in. It was an appendage to the Episcopal church next door where the bald-headed priest presided.

"Welcome, friends," Nathan extended his arms, ballet dancer–like, to Rush and me when we craned our heads into the living room. "And how is it with your spirits today?"

This is just the sort of unanswerable question facilitators like to ask each other. Nathan had mentored me through my training at the Quaker nonprofit.

I paused to notice. "Present? I think." I can never be sure. People assume that because I'm a writer, reflection comes easily, but I'm a writer because it does not. If there is any silver lining to the unknowing, it is this: a ragged curiosity that calls and does not quit.

Two other friends, Will and Juli, arrived soon after. I had sent out an e-mail a few weeks prior explaining the process. The ground rules for the Clearness Committee prohibited "fixing, saving, advising, or correcting" of any kind. If you wanted to help someone in this space, you did so by listening to them, or rather, listening to them listen to themselves aloud. In other words, you helped them by trying not to be too helpful. Quoting from my facilitator handout, I wrote, *The Clearness Committee is a testimony to the fact that there are*

no external authorities on life's deepest issues, not clergy or thera-
pists or scholars; there is only the authority that lies within each of
us waiting to be heard.[9]

The five of us made ourselves comfortable in the loosely arranged circle of sofas and armchairs. Rush chose the stiffest seat—beige, basket weave, all creak and no give. He shifted his weight, noisily, and winked at me. One of the earliest uses of the Clearness Committee was for couples discerning marriage; I was glad to have made peace with that imperfect institution, even as I was struggling to embrace another.

About adoption we had agreed: Either it was a yes from both of us or we would not do it. And if it was a no? We would not keep fostering. The on-ramp had been hard, long, bumpy. We were tired of filling potholes. It was forever children or never again children. From across the room, perched at the edge of a checkered couch, I winked back at Rush.

It was time.

We uncrossed our bobbing legs. We put pillows behind our tired backs. Nathan cleared his throat and started in on the first verse of a Denise Levertov poem: "Just when you seem to yourself nothing but a flimsy web of questions, you are given the questions of others to hold."[10]

I'm holding these questions now, literally, while I tarry over this part of the story. It's part of the process that while the focus persons externalize their insides, blessedly uninterrupted save for some gentle questions, the rest of the "committee" takes notes. Three neat piles of yellow-legal-pad paper are stapled together and sitting on my desk, the back of one bloodied from a mosquito I killed this morning.

I'm not sure what I expect to find, flipping through the stacks of handwritten scribbles. Some proof that we weren't fools? That we didn't miss some obvious and foreboding clue? Or maybe I expect something closer to an explanation. An explanation for why I said *yes* to motherhood? An explanation for what I'm doing, writing a book about making meaning beyond it?

I start with Will's notes, whose handwriting is neater, bigger, more cheerful than the others. Will is a friend from college. He has a kind face, big lips, wears khakis. Will sat in an overstuffed armchair and spoke with a tired kindness. If there were any nerves, and I imagine there were (I am always hoping to narrate things properly), his questions would have loosened my knots. Will puts his name at the top.

I move on to Nathan's handwriting: delicate, deep blue, small *g*'s like artful figure eights. Nathan has the widest, whitest smile of anyone you'll ever meet. He is fit, skin bright and healthy, posture upright and easy. That day, I remember how his clerical collar poked out of a black button-up tucked into blue jeans. He is always the picture of integrity, a picture that feels beyond my talents. I think I wore pleated sweatpants to the meeting.

I give up on Juli's handwriting: cherry red, shaky, like a doctor's prescription. I met Juli in graduate school. We ate lunch together on the utility stairs outside when the cafeteria was too noisy. Her gentle stare never rushed me to resolution, which was a fine trait to have during the Clearness Committee, in which two hours, excessive though it may have seemed to us at first, reliably slipped by. Her penmanship gives me a headache now, and I do not make it past the first page.

It's just as well. After a few fits and starts, I decide the answer is not in the answers. It's in the questions.

What do you want? What do you want for your people? Are there overlapping circles of desire?

What gifts would parenting affirm in you? What challenges would it mean? What emotions claw at you as you're considering?

When do you feel God most present?

What values do you want to guide the decision? When do you feel closest, farthest, to a decision?

Is there some third way you're not seeing, between adopting and never fostering again? Between having children and never having children at all?

I have often imagined that if I could remember whatever shred of clarity I had in that moment, then I would not be here excavating the past. If I could just remember what it felt like to stretch my legs after those two hours of sitting, to hug my friends in unspeakable gratitude, to get back in the car with Rush and drive toward a decision, then I would not be here trying to rewrite my life. I would not flop backward into the folds of our down comforter at the end of another endless day and plead with Rush, "What have we done, love?" If I could just remember what it felt like when I knew what I knew, I would be like Nathan, the picture of integrity.

So, would it sound like an ass-covering measure if I told you that the one true thing that came out of that day was a kind of faithfulness, faithfulness in listening to our inner teacher, our community, our God? Would you believe me if I told you that I'm a little giddy to find there were no clear answers, no missed clues? That it's a relief to know the questions were good ones, perennial ones?

It makes me think our questions are the most generous gifts we can give each other. Not our clarity. Not our well-groomed advice. Because the life well-lived has no experts. It has no shortcuts. It has always been a process rather than a product that can be bought and sold and put on a shelf. Faithfulness cannot be replicated, but the invitation to it can.

I know this in my bones.

My life is not an answer.

It is a question.

So, perhaps *that* is what I've been up to this whole time. Holding your questions. Trading you mine. Another silver lining to the unknowing.

The Salve for Regret

It's only now that I am mothering that other mothers whisper to me, "I think I would have been fine without." "I'm counting down the days until college." "No matter my 'village,' at the end of the day, it's just me. Telling him to take his meds." "Talking her off a ledge." "There is no life raft big enough."

In the cultural narrative I was handed, not-mothering was always posed as the biggest threat of regret. But what about mothering? Reliable statistics are hard to find, given that the assessment of motherly regret is both subjective and highly stigmatized. (According to some polls, maybe somewhere between 7 and 14 percent of parents?)[11] It's also not fixed to a set time period in a child's life, making its borders feel like smog, hazy and heavy.

Through a friend of a friend, one anonymous mother asks me where she can go for help, and I go to Google. Google produces a Facebook group called "I Regret Having Children" that has almost twenty-five thousand followers. Google produces a book called *Regretting Motherhood* that "asks honest and difficult questions about how society pushes women into motherhood." Google produces a magazine article, headline "Inside the Growing Movement of Women Who Wish They'd Never Had Kids." "I really didn't know what I was in for," says Laura, whose name has been changed.

Everyone's name has been changed in the piece.

It makes me wonder now, do I regret mothering? To be

honest, I am still having trouble admitting what exactly my regrets are, so indoctrinated have I been in the belief that looking back is dumb. And not just dumb but dangerous. One thinks of the biblical Lot's wife. While fleeing Sodom and Gomorrah, Lot's wife gets turned into a pillar of salt for disobeying an angel's orders to "flee for your life; do not look back or stop anywhere." And so when I start wrestling with my regrets—I regret trying to prove useful in the first place, I regret thinking three children would be no different than two, I regret privileging a private solution (to adopt or not) over a public problem (an epidemic of child abuse and neglect)—I, too, end up feeling consumed.

But to regret is human. This must be why we try so hard to avoid it; it reminds us of what we are. And, maybe, the only real hedge against it is to speak more honestly about our lives as they are and not as we wish them to be. To stop trying to advise the failure right out of one another. To listen for the peculiarities rather than the similarities in each other's stories. To wear regret like ashes on our foreheads, a reminder that we are not-God and regret is not the end.

To CONFESS REGRET from time to time then seems to me one salve for it. Rush confides on a windy walk that he is tired of people telling him that "what's in the past is in the past." "Right," I jump in, "because the past can teach us to do better." He shakes his head. "No, because sometimes you have to sit with the fact that there is no quick fix." He is telling me something important; I pull my hood over my pinked ears and listen.

Equally important then, I think, to confess where regret has not taken root. This is especially true when regret has been weaponized against you. And so I start ruminating on the things I don't regret—I don't regret never being pregnant alongside friends; I don't regret loving my work so much I skipped over loving small children; I don't regret at least asking how a private solution could ease a public problem.

Along with threatening our sense of belonging, regret is most intense in decisions that defy our justification or betray our values. Parenting may not always feel consistent with my personal values—simplicity, solitude, and intimacy have had to shape-shift while mothering—but it is consistent with a communal value to take care of who's here. Come to think of it, this communal value is the *only* reason I don't regret non-motherhood *or* motherhood writ large.

So, it's not that we *don't* need security for a life well-lived. We are wired to survive and, for much of human history, we've survived by sticking together. It's that we need security in a cultural narrative that is not contingent upon our ability to be fortune-tellers, insurance salesmen, or investment bankers, treating people like appreciating assets.

I had forgotten until recently that Jesus employs his own object lesson to make this same point. "Remember Lot's wife," he says, and I sigh. But after more than a cursory read, I don't think he's making a case against the examined life. I think he's making a case against looking for security in the wrong things. "Those who try to make their life secure will lose it, but those who lose their life will keep it."

OF COURSE, NONE of this means I don't still get wistful about what might have been if Rush and I had not said yes to parenting. (There is, if you must know, still much bed flopping at the end of the day.) But I am starting to think of these moments as glimpses of a sister life that is no longer mine to live.

Naturally, this gorgeous concept comes from a poet.

I stumble across it while reading Cheryl Strayed's beloved Dear Sugar column. A reader wants to know how one can know, really know, in the end if they will or won't regret children. She points them to Tomas Transtromer's poem "The Blue House," in which a man observes the architecture of his life as if he were a ghost, on the outside, peering in.

In that house with the misty blue walls, the man sees the outlines of all that has been and all that almost was. He, like me, tries to imagine what it felt like before the not-so-inevitabilities felt so inevitable. He, like me, is trying to be grateful, all while admitting he misses the alternatives. His salve then, if you can call it that, comes from not only confessing regret, but also releasing his regrets into the forgiving sea. He writes, "We don't really know it, but we sense it: there is a sister ship to our life which takes a totally different route."[12]

So this is it then. This is exactly the metaphor I've needed to get on with savoring my life; a nautical reminder that I can't chart every life. For heaven's sake, I can't even chart the hundred I once dreamed of, although there is much to be said for trying to read or write your way into a few more possibilities. I can see now that this is the end I've been navigating toward all along. This is a way to hail both the childfree life that might have been and the childfull one that is now chugging onward.

Now, maybe you have faith in something more orthodox than me. Maybe my jubilant use of poetry is too much for you. None of this matters to me at the moment. Because, in this moment, it makes sense to me. And, given that I have no literary criticism skills to speak of, I feel infinite freedom to ask not what the poet meant, but what the poem means for me. Waving goodbye to my sister ship both liberates me and creates unfathomable room in me.

I think my sister ship is a cruise liner.

Maybe this is but one way to lose your life and find another.

The Decision Has Been Made

So, we were saying yes to the adoption.

We were saying yes because we had an imagination for yes. No felt like it would return us to the life we knew. It didn't have to be that way, mind you, but we could not think of a single want or dream or vision to embellish upon that could not include the girls. Was this exhaustion or insight? To say no would be to say yes to a yet-formed idea. To say yes was to say yes to already-present people. We were working on privileging the present.

We were saying yes because while we believed either decision was fine (fine but not right; right is a rare and rigid thing), we were still committed to privileging the vulnerable in our community. I still wasn't especially comfortable with "the vulnerable" as a category. I still wasn't especially comfortable with children. But I liked Youngest and the way her nose flattened when she smiled, and I liked Middle and how she whined "Wh-ay?" in her corny, Southern kid voice, and I liked Oldest for asking the neighbor for an iron whenever I was too shy.

We were saying yes because we thought we could be good for the girls and they could be good for us. The Clearness Committee had helped us reframe our original choice: to adopt the girls or never foster again. We left that time with a new question, "Was there a third way?" We did not know exactly what that looked like yet. (We would ask the therapists.) But perhaps it meant thinking of ourselves more as guardians than gatekeepers. We would hold these children for safekeeping until they could sort out for themselves to whom and how they would belong.

These were only the outlines of our yes. As clear as we were sometimes (and to be sure we were clearest when not actively parenting), the reasons behind the decision were anything but. Still, I read the words of Clarissa Pinkola Estés in book club and understood that there were other choices, more important choices, to consider now, like "whether to be bitter or not." I decided I would not.

And then I would decide again.

Our ship had sailed.

CHAPTER 8

Script: Family Is the Greatest Legacy

Rewrite: Legacy Is So Much More Than DNA

Go and bear fruit—fruit that will last.
—Jesus[1]

AFTER THE DECISION, there was a steady stream of paperwork.

By January 2017, we knew that the termination of parental rights had not been appealed. We knew that we were the only adoptive parents being considered. We knew that the legal process would take another two to four months. (It ended up taking six.) Things were moving swiftly, by government standards.

Step 1 in the legal process was hiring an attorney; our new adoptive social worker gave us the option of using a government-approved one or hiring our own. Given that I was still using my best friend from high school's husband—a San Francisco–based lawyer who specialized in green energy—to review book contracts, we opted for the government-approved option.

The government-approved option was also, conveniently, free. This was shocking to me; the few times I'd asked friends if they had ever considered adoption, cost was almost always cited as one of the obstacles. Now, I wondered if they had had in their minds only infants, or only adoptions from faraway places. Or perhaps cost was a cover for a deeper fear. I couldn't be sure of their reasonings. (I was still sorting through mine.) But after doing the yearly budget, I reckoned that we'd saved somewhere north of six thousand dollars in legal fees. The penny-pincher in me—the one who tracks every crumbled receipt in a color-coded spreadsheet—rejoiced.

Then came Step 2. The girls would be issued new birth certificates, with our names, their names, and every detail about their entry into the world erased save for the date. It was a savagely ahistorical practice, in my opinion. Rush had already shut down my idea to protest by changing *our* last names to theirs. But what of changing *their* last names to ours?

We had talked some over the years about naming conventions, should we have the children we didn't planning on having. "The first one can have my name, so as to properly set social expectations. Then the next one can have yours, and so on and so forth," I'd proposed. We had tried this strategy with Amelia's surname—changing it every time we moved vets—and the confusion, the inequity, never bothered us, or her.

But children are not pets. I know this. There is a case to be made for renaming. But given that our girls had lived with their first names for some time, and their last names were tied to their cultural identity, we left them. Instead, we opted to bequeath them middle names, Latin names inspired by our Anglo grandmothers. For the next few years, we will receive desperate texts around the holidays, asking how exactly to address our crew. One friend will be so brilliant as to mash up the first two letters of each of our surnames, thereby rendering us Italianate.

For help with Step 3, we would need a Realtor. We wanted a new house, a house that belonged to all five of us. (For this reason, we wanted a new puppy, too; Amelia was gracious to the girls but squarely preferred us.) So, we started looking for something in Raleigh, with the idea that a bit of physical and psychological distance from Durham might help a fresh start.

Our housing requirements were specific: more square footage but not more than we could keep clean, a functional kitchen but not one that had been flipped (the finishings were never right), and a closed floor plan. I'd watched enough home shows to know that the open floor plan was the stuff of parental fetish. "We want to keep an eye on the kids," people liked to say. *Yes, but doesn't this mean they can keep on eye you?* I wondered. A few walls still sounded nice to me, to be able to move around nimbly, unbidden.

Oh, and in the spirit of my mother, we required a basement, a basement where kids could go to be kids and, one day, guests could return to being guests. Just guests.

Rush and I had become parents out of principle: We wanted to be a part of a communal project of care. What we didn't expect was how good it would feel to start caring as particular *somebodies'* parents. To pick out a pair of butterfly bell bottoms that fit. To write a measured note to the teacher who spits "tattletale." To decide it was okay for kids to sing "fuck that shit" along with Wiz, so long as they didn't sing along at school. The writer in me loved to cluck, "There are no bad words, only bad usages." Whether I was starting to see the appeal of parenting or just desperate to wrest a bit of control, it's hard to say. All I knew is that for the first time in more than a year, it felt like we were making plans without God laughing.

We still clung to our great many principles, like the superpower of unlikely families or how one needn't be called Mom or Dad to impact children. We certainly didn't need to call our children *daughters*. And we told people so. Well, I told people so. I told people that I preferred to call them "our girls," that they were already somebody's daughters, that I didn't need them to be mine.

So, when Oldest's therapist suggested that we begin, tentatively, using the term, I pushed back with all my principles. She agreed with my principles. And she reminded me that kids don't care about principles. They care how they fit into reality as it is, not reality as we believe it should be. They care, almost obnoxiously, about belonging.

It was on our one-year move-in anniversary that we tried the word for the first time. The girls begged to celebrate at a hibachi buffet in Durham, where they loaded their plates with monochromatic combinations of lo mein, mac and cheese, and mashed potatoes that had the texture of wet concrete. There, the three of them smooshed in a green pleather booth, we told them that no matter how they thought of us, we would always think of them as, *gulp*, daughters.

It was uncomfortable telling them something we weren't sure had to be said and, maybe, they weren't sure they wanted to hear. But I noticed Oldest relax in the days after we uttered it. Her hugs felt less bony. Her tears flowed more freely. And I felt in those moments that she was becoming not more mine but more herself.

Beloved.

Social Legacy

It's been ten months since I last drove to Durham. The drive is familiar. Past the airport where, not certain what young children liked to do, I once took the girls to watch planes take off from the observation park. Past the columned courthouse in which Rush and I sat, complicit in our ill-fitting slacks in an ill-fitting system. Past the house where we used to live and the yellow door with the devious grin.

Today, I've made a date to talk legacy with Jeanette. Jeanette is my oldest friend in town. She's not the oldest in the sense that I've known her the longest, though I found her during my first semester of graduate school. She's the oldest in numerical age at sixty-eight; she still works doggedly at an old corner grocer she converted into an office. It's here, in an argentine bungalow with an aluminum awning, where she runs the Resource Center for Women & Ministry in the South or, as I prefer to call it, the Resource Center for Women & Mischief.

Its origin story has all the markings of a superhero saga. It was the 1970s, and small-boned but smart-mouthed Jeanette was among the first women to enroll at Duke Divinity School because she wanted to talk about politics, theology, and suffering—you know, she recalled, the whole "Why are there starving children in India?" question. She just had no earthly clue how to turn talking into a living. A mentor suggested, "Why don't you do something nobody else is going to do?"

Jeanette started by listening. After graduating, she went around asking her woman friends who were on the front lines of local church ministry what it was that they needed. What they needed, they reported, was connection. They wanted to know someone cared that they existed and talk to others who knew that existence was hard. So, determined to fight the twin villains of isolation and "The Man," Jeanette found a tax lawyer, bought a cardboard card file, and started collecting names for a newsletter that would become the hallmark of her newly minted nonprofit.

If a tax lawyer, a card file, and a newsletter are not the stuff of legends, I don't know what is.

THE WORDS LEGENDS and *legacy* share the same root, *leg,* meaning to collect or gather. The word *legal* is also included in this etymological family. If, when we talk about legacy, we are talking about who will inherit your collection of antique tea-cups or the signed, first-edition, mystery novels you've gathered over the years, I am not all that interested in the concept.

Around my house, I have a reputation as a heartless thrower-awayer of things. Unmatched socks. Unloved toys. Unremarkable notes or hand-drawn art. Call it a lack of sentimentality or a failure to imagine the future, but I am not compelled by keepsakes. Once, Youngest gave me a coupon book that gifted me the ability to toss two of her "nicknacs," so well-known is my pulverizing joy.

This kind of thinking extends to my own terrestrial im-mortality. I don't need my name etched into a building. Or even a stone to mark my grave. Do I even need a grave? "Do what you want with me," I've told Rush flatly. "According to the Bible, marriage isn't even a thing in heaven." It's true. The Christian tradition is a bit of a buzzkill about earthly attach-ments, including familial ones, and for some reason, it gives me some pleasure telling people so.*

Maybe I like this theology so very much because women without children are sometimes made to worry about what,

---

* For instance, Jesus was once asked by a group of Sadducees about a woman who was widowed seven times, by seven brothers, none of whom she had children with. At the resurrection, which of the seven brothers would be her husband? they wanted to know. Surely, we couldn't all die and come back from the dead without some major legal head-aches. Who would we belong to? Simple, Jesus said. Like the angels, who according to the scriptures are not subject to death and therefore not subject to marriage (with its emphasis on sex, birth, and heirs), we'll belong to God. Or, in the spirit of saint Maya Angelou, we'll belong to everyone and no one at all.

or more specifically *who*, they will leave behind. For much of human history, this anxiety was compounded by illiteracy. "For one's name to live on after one's death, there had to be someone to keep it alive."[2] Especially for ancient Near Eastern women, who were not riding headlong into battle or negotiating treaties that would be etched into history, children were the primary way to achieve immortality. They were the primary way to cement meaning.

Centuries of progress have gifted women, especially well-educated White women like Jeanette and me, other ways to leave our handprints in the sidewalk. But when the topic turns to legacy, much of the current conversation *still* turns to one's children, only now it's less centered on children as vessels of memory (inventions like the printing press, cameras, and the Internet prove useful here) but vessels of morality.

Perhaps you've heard some version of these truisms. Legacy is not "for our children but in our children." Legacy is not "something you do but someone you raise." Legacy is not about passing on money (or mystery novels) to your children and grandchildren but values and faith. More than some, I think, I can appreciate this focus off stuff and onto substance. I can also appreciate how it valorizes a historically feminine offering—the formation of the next generation—and gives it equal, if not more, worth than the grand gestures, shrewd politics, or uncompromising productivity so commonly praised in men.

However. Whatever the legacy being praised, the subtext of the question remains the same. Children are the assumed *who* that we live our lives for and leave our lives to. They are the things that carry us, like messages in green-glass bottles, bobbing unevenly toward some unknown shore, trying not to sink with the weight of our hopes.

SITTING AT THE round kitchen table in the back of the one-room Resource Center where boxes of tea and bars of chocolate are arranged neatly on open shelves, I wonder how Jeanette is thinking of her legacy, given the fact that she hasn't the vessel of biological children.

"Well, my cousins populate half the state of Texas, if you work at it, and a big chunk of North Carolina, too," she informs me, putting one tiny hand on top of the other, before adding pertly, "and that's a legacy. It's not my legacy, but there are lots of ways to leave a legacy."

"So, what kind of legacy are you leaving?" I goad, unwrapping a gold-foil square of toffee and popping it into my mouth; after ten years of friendship, the answer to this question is so obvious to me that I zone out for a few seconds while I let the waxy sweetness cover my teeth.

Jeanette's legacy is what's called a *social legacy*, a term used to describe the way in which one can meaningfully influence people not just in one's own family, or one's family line, but in one's community. You might say a social legacy is about gathering people who share a duty to one another rather than

DNA with one another. You might say it looks a lot like a cardboard card file.

Jeanette thinks about my question for a moment. She tucks her long, wiry hair behind one ear, then another, before finally offering, "Well, I'm leaving a legacy of the people I've had relationships with." This includes the smart, athletic woman she dated during her thirties who never wanted to parent. Then there was the man she married at thirty-eight with whom she tried to get pregnant and got early menopause instead. This includes the man she married at fifty-six—the man she's married to now—the man who came with two children from a previous marriage. "They have a completely functional mother," she says, and "I didn't need to replace her."

Of course, her relational legacy extends beyond her romantic past. She mentions the books she's written (six so far), the political activity she's been involved with (in the seventies she organized around the Equal Rights Amendment; now it's voter registration drives and anti-racism trainings), and the institution she grew that had, in her words, "some influence." The handwritten collection of names that began forty years ago has turned into an e-mail list of thousands—and a staff of four. Their desks hug the perimeter of the room; stacks of papers portend upcoming events; thumbtacked scraps capture moments past: a writing workshop, an art opening, one photo shows a young girl in a straw hat and dinosaur top.

The girl in the photo is almost four years old now. She belongs to the Resource Center's Director of Development;

Jeanette has had a grand time following her around the office since she was born. (Each time I visit, the child is mentioned through no effort of mine.) It surprises Jeanette that she has no grandchildren by now; she'd always assumed she'd become a mother and, consequently, a grandmother. One of her stepchildren may have a child eventually, she muses. In the meantime, she is finding herself drawn to women in their thirties, women who are the same age a daughter of hers might be.

I'm puzzled then, given her complete devotion to the Resource Center and its complete dependency on her, that she seems ambivalent about her non-procreative legacy. At one point during our conversation, she clears her throat before confiding, "I can't tell you how many friends I have with grandchildren who say to younger women, 'Don't have children.' I mean, it's heartbreak, among other things, among many other things." But later, she admits, "I feel a little bit sad for the older women I know who were never married and don't have children." She's concerned that they won't have anyone to take care of them as they age. She wonders who is going to take care of her. "So I will just keep making friends," she offers, her Southern lilt softening, "in hopes that somebody will come and visit me."

Jeanette is onto something, I think. I've been reading about how friendships are one of the most essential (and underrated) ingredients in a life well-lived. Friendships have a bigger impact on health and well-being than family. Friendships rank inordinately high on our pleasure scales. In fact, in one ongoing study, parents ranked time with friends higher in enjoyment than time with spouses, relatives, acquaintances, and one's own parents.[3] (Time with one's children came in on par with time with strangers.) Friendships can even help women live longer and age easier. Odd then that so much energy is still put on pouring into our familial legacy when the effects of friendship, friendships like Jeanette's and mine, may be not only more rewarding but more enduring.

"Okay, one final question," I promise Jeanette, tossing another row of chocolate into my canvas tote for the road. She nods her silent approval for me to continue. "I'm curious. If you could film a thirty-second PSA about your life, what would you want others to know?"

"There's nothing missing," she says, almost instantly. "I've been to Nepal, but I have not, quote, climbed Mount Everest, and there are other people who have." She pauses, her sharp chin lifted. "I *may* be a lesser human being for never having the total responsibility of a tiny person. But there's no way to know that."

I replay her words on my drive home. Past the house where, if the girls had moved out, we might have hosted another neighbor, a tired refugee, an aging parent. *But there's no way to know that.* Past the courthouse where I might have volunteered to be a guardian ad litem, to advocate for families instead of raising my own. *But there's no way to know that.* Past the airport where I might have been the person in the sky right now rather than the one headed homeward.

Housewarming

We got the call that the adoption was official three carts deep in the Ikea storeroom. Rush and Oldest and I were there hunting area rugs. Our bodies instinctively bowed toward one another in a group hug. The moment was as all life-changing moments are: blink-fast and fluorescent. No more than five minutes later, we were waiting in the checkout line and weighing whether to get food court meatballs.

We shared the news with the younger girls when we returned to our house in Durham, which was now all boxes and bare floors. Middle put her hands on her dimpled cheeks and screamed. Youngest let her face fall as the finality sunk in. But seeing her big sisters celebrate—even Oldest, who so often refused—opened up a pocket of permission in her. Soon, Youngest was looking up at us with wide eyes and repeating over and over again, "Now I have two dads! Now I have two moms!"

The final stretch of legal hurdles had been remarkably smooth. And, again, *we didn't have to pay a cent;* monthly adoption assistance payments would continue until the girls were eighteen, and a yearly pot of money was available to cover ongoing needs for things like therapy, educational testing, and day camps with floppy-haired counselors named Jack. If I was ever going to become a parent in modern-day America, this was the way I wanted it: consensual, communal, subsidized. This is the way I want it for all parents, mind you.

One week later, we moved to Raleigh. Our new house was better than I hoped. It was another hundred-year-old bungalow, heaven help us, with squeaky floors and walls enough. Unpainted cedar-plank boards wrapped the kitchen ceiling. Floating stairs lead down to a basement with exposed brick and concrete floors. Our neighbors were near; out the front door was the downtown skyline, out the back a state prison. It was perfect. It made me feel like just the sort of person I still imagined myself to be.

We unpacked quickly, though not as quickly as we had when it was only Rush and me. There were more interruptions. The girls insisted on eating at regular intervals. I insisted that everything in their rooms have a home. "It doesn't have to be its home forever," I said of the framed photo of their birth family or, say, the framed photo of a lemur, "but it needs to have a place where it belongs."

Home had started out as a symbol of my autonomy. It signified that I was rid of my dad's habit of never unpacking. Or my mom's indiscriminate hospitality. I could finally buy nice things, color-code my library, build a world *without* words for once. It was the place where I went inside myself to be most myself by myself. And it was still this place in some ways. I was still this person, only now with a little more adeptness at sharing. It was a day of great personal growth when I let Oldest get the mail.

A new home then, one in which five people could be their

own people, together, felt like the thing to throw a party over. Not the adoption. Not the entry into motherhood. "Come celebrate our new roof" the invitation read, even though I was beginning to think rooflessness was closer to the human condition.

The party was on a Saturday. People came from all over. Our parents came. Charlie would come a week later because the airfare was cheaper. The two godparents we'd handpicked for Youngest came. When we'd discovered that Youngest didn't have any *padrinos*—and it meant something to the older two that they did—we took it upon ourselves to find her some. I convinced Rush, though it didn't take much, to choose two childless women, unrelated to each other.

It was a message I hoped would one day sink in with my three girls: The ability or intent or desire to procreate has no bearing on how blessed you are, or how good you are, or how you can embody the image of love, the image of God, for someone else. Having a child does not automatically make saints out of sinners, nor does remaining childless shrivel saints into shrews. Parenting of any kind is a crucible, sure, but so is writing a book. So is surviving a life.

The housewarming was merry, quirky. The first guests who arrived brought a linen pillow that read "Established 2017." The girls, honestly, loved it. I don't remember if we prayed—audibly. Maybe I was already feeling at capacity, what with all the people and crumbs. Children—other people's children—played in the backyard. A new record played on the console. Amelia played, reluctantly, with the new puppy, her big brown eyes pleading, "Is this really my life now?"

"Yes, this is really our life now," I told her.

Spiritual Legacy

In appearance, I have a different life than the one I intended. But, looking back, I want to argue that maybe it's not so far off. Maybe what I've always wanted, more than anything, is to measure my life not by its outward signs of success but by an alternative kind of legacy. It's just that sometimes this legacy comes disguised in the trappings of family—a house, a marriage, daughters.

We get hung up on the trappings of a life and miss the deep desire of a life.

Christians get hung up on the original command to "be fruitful and multiply." We say *make babies, make nations, make something of yourself, fill the world with something of yourself, because this is how the world will not forget you or your God.* If influence is the measure of worth, then multiplying your genes, your beliefs, is a hell of a good way to prove it.

But, now hear me out, what if legacy is not actually meant to *prove* anything?

Christians get so hung up on the original command that we often miss the new command—or is it really just the same blessing phrased differently?—to "go and bear fruit—fruit that will last." It's a sentiment that comes in the thick of

Jesus's farewell address. He's contemplating his own legacy. And he essentially says, *I'm like a vine and you're like its branches, you're only as fruitful as the source you're connected to, we're only as fruitful as our ability to abide with each other.* Resting in love, the scripture says, is the only way to multiply love.

Which means, if the metaphor holds, legacy is not about proving. It's not about producing. Not children. Not books. It's about resting in the sweetness of a life that was never mine alone to decide. It's one of my few certainties: Whether my life bears fruit—and fruit that will last—is not really up to me. It's for others, which is also to say God, to prune and ripen.

I want to call this undeserved yield a *spiritual legacy*.

So, here is what I propose: What if the ultimate question of a life well-lived is not, *How will I make my mark?* but instead, *Who will I be marked by?*

I have been marked. I have been marked by Janell and her legacy of the "fierce inventory." I have been marked by Lisa and a neighborliness that defies class comforts. Margaret has marked me with her breathing space. So, too, have I been marked by Jessica and Shalom and Becky and their liberating mothering. Karen and Melody marked me with their good and grand questions and Iris with her reminder that "it's not who you love but how you love." Sarah marked me with her capacity to care for what doesn't come assigned to us. Em marked me with her ability to speak the truth, speaking only for herself. I will forevermore be marked by Jeanette and her legacy of a tax lawyer, a card file, and a newsletter. Newsletters widen our ecosystem of belonging.

A social or spiritual legacy, whatever you want to call it, is not always as singular as a familial one. I get that. And for that reason, I think, it can be tricky to spot and savor. Children may not rank among the most enjoyable company but they are overwhelmingly cited by parents as the most fulfilling.[4] Not to mention that they are awfully good at dressing up life's natural boredom and giving it some shine. They made my life very shiny at the time of the adoption and that shine cued the applause of others. I don't blame them; I am grateful for the casseroles. I understand this now: Life, wherever it is found on display, is dazzling.

So, here is my solemn vow: I will look for the dazzle in the dimmer milestones. I vow to mark not just births but new beginnings; I vow to participate in the baptism of not just babies but vocations; I vow to throw down for not just graduations but the gradual tides of aging. And this vow, this vow of attention to how women are making, and have always been making, meaning beyond the bright lights of motherhood, will be how I make my peace.

Good for You

A year and a half after my initial interrogation of her, Janell returns to Raleigh for twenty-four hours. She is here for the inaugural "Good for You" dinner.

A few months prior, a friend from church named Steve had asked me, "If you were to throw a dinner in honor of some unseen group of people, who would it be?"

"That's easy," I said between slurps of iced tea. "I would honor women who are biologically childfree." His face remained unchanged. "You know," I continued, "women who aren't sad or mad about not procreating?"

He considered the category. "But do you think there are even thirty of them in Raleigh?"

I spit my Sencha out. "Steve! You know these women. Your pastor is these women."

The invitations proved impossible to word. Did I mean to exclude women who had given birth? Did I mean to include women who had children living under their roof? Were adoptive mothers truly in the same lane as never-mothers? It was a puzzle. No matter how many times I tried rearranging the pieces (I know! I'll add an asterisk!) I couldn't convince others, let alone myself, of where the edges lay. In the end, eighteen women agreed to the imperfect ask, including Janell, who has flown in from Denver just for this dinner, just for me.

The night feels like a wedding, but instead of one couple promising a private love, it's fistfuls of women committing to doing the communal work of discerning, fashioning, and savoring a life well-lived. Four long tables, teeming with hydrangeas, are set up in Steve's living room like we're at a banquet. A chef is in the kitchen, tall and ruddy, placing salmon onto pillows of couscous. A bartender stands behind a glass table, offering a signature cocktail. We dub it Blessed Be the Fruit. I am so flush with spirits and drunk with love for everyone there—I pinch myself when Janell ends up seated across from Pastor Lisa—that I leave hardly any time at all to facilitate the conversation I had planned.

By the time Janell and I get home and change into our hoodies, back at the dining room table dissecting the evening's unfolding, I am full. Full of gratitude but also full of longing, wishing there had been *more*. More conversations about who shaped our desire to mother or not. More about what we feel and what we're supposed to feel about children. More about how we find community when we find ourselves outside of convention. More, in the spirit of Audre Lorde, about how we can learn to mother ourselves.[5] In fact, after going over the small catalog of things I wish I'd done differently in the planning, this is my one takeaway. There is so much *more*.

A few days later I post an invitation to a monthly "Good for You" meetup at Em's downtown boutique for any woman who is making meaning beyond motherhood, whatever that means to her. I am floored by the responses. One woman wonders if she is missing the mom gene. (She's not. Remember: It doesn't exist.) Another says she craves non-mom groups but doesn't know of any in her neck of the woods. A handful say they feel like imposter moms—stepmoms, foster moms, and unlikely moms—who are not exactly childless but are not exactly in childlove. Others ask: When are you going to do something for moms who want to be celebrated as more than moms? There is so much *more*.

Which reminds me of a Hebrew word, *dayenu*, that means, "It would have been enough," or, literally, "enough for us." It's sung during Passover to remind the Jewish people that God's presence with them through slavery (*enough for us*), through wilderness (*enough for us*), through promised land (*enough for us*), is sufficient cause for awe. Anything more—and there has always been more—is absurd blessing. I wish I had sung this over Janell before she left for her after-midnight flight. I am not waiting for you to be useful to this world in some specific way beyond what you already are or may become. Your mere presence with me, yes, your hard-won, long-practiced, abiding presence, would have been enough.

And yet, inconceivably, you are so much more.

CHAPTER 9

Script: You Don't Know Love Until You Become a Mother

Rewrite: There Are Limitless Ways to Love to Your Limit

*[Love is] . . . profound concern for the well-being of another,
without any desire to control that other, to be thanked by that
other, or to enjoy the process.*

—Edward Nason West[1]

Is it abundantly clear by now? This book, my search, has been flawed from the start. One cannot consider how to love and be loved as "someone other than a mother" without inadvertently centering motherhood.

The challenge is a linguistic one. A single woman might be called a spinster. A married woman remains a wife. But there's no noun for a woman who doesn't rest her identity on a lack or love of children. (Even the terms used throughout this book—*childless, childfree,* my own clunky contribution of *childfull*—put the relationship to children at the fore.) The only positive suggestion I came across, coincidentally in a book attempting to reclaim the word *spinster,* was the phrase "ambiguous woman."[2] Literary scholar Carolyn Heilbrun first used the term in the 1980s to describe women who didn't center their lives on a man. Some decades later, I wanted to amend the definition to include women who didn't center their lives on children. However, when I tried the admittedly ambiguous term out on friends, they despised it, uniformly. Janell said, and I quote, "Eew."

One solution to this challenge is to reject its premise entirely. The word for a woman who doesn't rest her identity on a lack or love of children is *woman* or, better yet *human*. That women are counted as a separate category of human beings, "the second sex" according to Simone de Beauvoir, remains the central slight to be overcome. And it is not easily overcome. "There is no good answer to how to be a woman," concurs Rebecca Solnit in her book of essays *The Mother of All Questions*. "The art may instead lie in how we refuse the question."[3] I admire this refusal. And given that, from a theological standpoint, I'm keen to believe that there will not be women as we know women in the afterlife, I think this refusal points us in the direction of liberation. The question then of whether one finds meaning in motherhood or in spite of motherhood is rendered backward, boring. Meaning can be found everywhere and nowhere at all.

Another solution to the linguistic challenge is to insist that we are all mothers. Instead of seeing all women as human, all humans are cast as parents, with varying degrees of femininity emphasized. This approach appears, perhaps surprisingly, in both queer and Christian accounts of mothering. In some queer accounts, mothering is a political action that can be performed by any*body*, regardless of gender identity. "Love by any means necessary," the editors of *Revolutionary Mothering* call it. Likewise, in Christian accounts, God is considered the ultimate expression of this love, and so mothering becomes a divine action that can be performed by *any*body, regardless of human biology. (Julian of Norwich famously construed Jesus as our "true Mother in whom we are endlessly born and out of whom we shall never come."[4]) I admire this inclusivity, too. It gives those who want to mother but are often denied the shine of traditional motherhood, like the transgender housemother or the childless godmother, a way to see their work as something close to glorious, too.

Both the refusal and inclusion solutions share, I think, a similar aim to mine: to soften the false binary between the childless and childfull, moms and non-moms, women and not women. There is much I'm still learning from these thinkers. Where I want to stake my hope is in a linguistic solution, one that holds our impressive ideological aspirations with the material conditions of women's lives. While writing this book, two events took place that supersized this desire. One, a global pandemic devastated the planet and, subsequently, mothers. And two, a childless stepmother became the first woman vice president of the United States.

Mother or Mother Superior, Reprise

Before the pandemic, for the first time in almost a decade, women made up a greater percentage of the American job market than men.[5] Whatever one thinks of a woman's place, the benefits of paid work are hard to knock, especially when that paid work is essential in meeting our basic needs for reliable food, housing, and healthcare. Paid work can also be pretty damn gratifying, putting value to brow-sweating effort or long-unsung talent. Three weeks before the country locked down, I accepted an offer to publish this book after years of writing—and rewriting—the proposal alone. For a brief time, my mental health soared.

Then the news. A mysterious virus was forcing my children's schools to close for two weeks. To be safe, we canceled our spring break plans, too. Amelia went on a hunger strike and died before Easter. We were gutted of our favorite coparent. More news. Schools were shuttered for the remainder of the year. Bahaha! I texted Rush from the bedroom where I worked with the door closed and the sound machine on "wind tunnel." How naive we'd been to think we could skip our way past the stay-at-home parent stage.

I was one of the privileged ones. I did not lose my book contract. Rush did not lose his job. Our children were older and able, remarkably, to self-manage. Where they could not manage, Rush filled in; we agreed my work required more solitude. There were some days when I did not see a child until noon. I stopped exercising and started drinking two jars of wine nightly, but I was still fundamentally okay. We donated a portion of every stimulus check to make sure others not included in the federal relief packages were okay, too.

But many others, especially many American mothers, were *not* okay: "Almost 1 million mothers left the workforce during the pandemic, with Black mothers, Hispanic mothers and single mothers among the hardest hit."[6] Mothers who continued to work, whether on the front lines of care or from the confines of home, were likely to face daily threats of guilt, burnout, and "this is not what I signed up for"-level scorn. Meanwhile, the country continued to cast communal responsibilities as personal choices, spurring a new diagnosis of "decision fatigue." (To send to school or become a school? To find a job or give up on jobs?) At the time of this writing, women make up the same share of the labor force that they did in the late 1980s; many analysts blame the special strain on working moms.[7]

In other words, the pandemic shattered the illusion that if you are a mother, you can also and easily be "someone other." Childless friends confided in me that never had they felt so grateful for the relative freedom and quietude of their lives.

Childless women were ostensibly given more reason to rejoice when Kamala Harris, a stepmother without biological children, was elected vice president of the United States. For many reasons, hormonal and political, I was a steady leak of tears throughout the inauguration. So were other writers and commentators who described feeling validated upon seeing a woman, and a woman of color at that, depart from the hallowed mother scripts to fulfill the second-highest office in the land. They liked that she didn't bemoan her lack of biological children. They liked that she was ambitious, having donned impressive titles like attorney general of California and United States senator. Still, they liked that she celebrated her title of *Momala*, the title her stepchildren had given her, as "the one that means the most to me."[8]

Harris had exceeded a number of expectations over the course of her career while meeting one of the most basic: She insisted her maternal role was the most important. And it very well may be.

But savvy commentators noted that maternity has long been used as a bid for political sympathy, from the early suffragists who argued that giving women voting rights would "double the power of the home" to the Portland "Wall of Moms" who used their bodies as a barricade against police violence, because, in the words of one organizer, "Who wants to shoot a mom? No one."[9, 10] The assumption is that moms are worth more than non-moms. The assumption is that moms have more to lose than non-moms.

So, it's easy to understand why, in the wake of this political history, childless women might defend themselves against accusations that they are cold, unrelatable, unworthy even, by emphasizing how much they really do love children. Was this partly why some women at the Good for You dinner, when asked how they most wanted to be celebrated, mentioned relationships to nieces and nephews, mentees and students? To prove that they were not the worst thing a woman could be, that they were not unacceptably female? (*Erin, nobody is thinking about this stuff as much as you*, I hear Rush in my ear.)

In any case, the election once again shattered the illusion that if you are *not* a mother, you, too, can easily exist as "someone other." Either children were your world, or the world was your children.

And there again were the familiar options in sharp relief: Mother or Mother Superior.

The Mother of All Scripts

It is entirely possible, *probable* even, that a lot of women really do love children. Or really do love being a mother, more than anything. There is much to love. It's like the liberal arts major of a liberal arts degree. You think a lot about how to think. You learn a little about everything: geodes, ADHD, what sloths eat. You study at the feet of public schoolteachers. It's brilliant when parenting becomes a portal and not a wall to community.

As a young girl, my desire to be "whoever it was that I was" was never a wholesale rejection of motherhood—or mothers. I adored my mother and her adoration of me. I was very concerned about the world's children, both the breathing and unborn. Accompanying my "want ad" for a future husband was even an imagination for future children.

I had forgotten this until recently, when I pulled out a sixth-grade paper titled, "Dreams for the Future." In it, I am a soap opera star with "a smashing career" who commutes from the New Jersey suburbs. My husband is, like my own mother once was, a part-time nurse who cares for our three children. "Whenever the kids get a boo-boo, he will know what to do," I assure my readers, in case they are worried. I must sense that people worry.

I can see now that I have always been experimenting with how to write an alternative story about womanhood that can account for those like me: dramatic, pragmatic, happy to delegate need. Only by writing my way through *this* story have I been able to see that what I've long wanted to reject is not the fact that being a mother—biological or otherwise—can be meaningful, but the persistent belief that motherhood is a superior source of meaning, identity, and love to all the others.

There is no social script that captures this myth better than *You don't know love until you become a mother.* Every mother script I ever inherited logically leads to this one: Motherhood is inevitable (script #1), dutiful (script #2), occupational (script #3), conventional (script #4), principal (script #5), instinctual (script #6), rational (script #7), memorial (script #8), and now exceptional (script #9). Motherhood, the logic goes, is so exceptional that until you experience it, you are a shell of human capacity. Again, a prepubescent version of who you could be: small-minded, underdeveloped, and not just a little bit narcissistic.

I see some version of this script paging through celebrity interviews in magazines, scrolling through inspirational quote plates on Instagram, reading articles from glowing, earthy mamas. Before motherhood, you are swimming in the shallows. After motherhood, you are drowning in the sacred. Before, your love was an abstraction. After, it is ruthlessly present. Before, your love kept a ledger. After, it is scrubbed clean of conditions. This is just how it is for mothers. This is how you know you're a mother. *Honey*, you'll understand when you're a mother. Because according to the gushing gurus, mother love isn't just expansive. It's exclusive, like a seat at the adult's table or a first-class ticket to enlightenment.

As a mother myself now, allow me to suggest that this is some hot, unholy garbage.

Now, my body was never bathed in pregnancy hormones, and my children never spat cute profundities to me from a car seat, and I understand if that means I am not entirely a reliable source on these things, but who are these usually decent people to make a gate out of love? To think that it's any more sacred to rinse your baby's patchy, thin hair in the sink than your mother's? That it requires any more presence to receive your child's vulnerable and ill-timed disclosures than your friend's? That it's any purer to love a teenager who breaks your heart over and over again than it is to do the same for your own sorry self? Are these alternative loves so very crude or inconceivable? Or is it more crude, more inconceivable, to look a woman in her stupid, gorgeous face and say, unequivocally, "You don't know love . . ."?

Look, I can't refute that those who subscribe to this script have indeed experienced a love like no other for their children. (This is, of course, the problem. The argument is set up in such a way that it cannot be refuted.) Because, in fact, there is no earthly way for me to know what others experience as love. Is it the good ache you get in your chest? Or the knowing goosebumps that grow on your arms? Maybe it's more like an orgasm, an irrepressible urge from the inside to quake, whether in ecstasy or fear, communion or self-actualization, that for one blessed gasp empties you of all ego?

People, my point is that there is no way for me to know what you know as love. And there is no way for you to know what I know as love. And so, without the very important subject switch from "*You* don't know love until you become a mother" to "*I* didn't know love until I became a mother," it is an awfully bold statement with an awfully death-dealing subtext: "You *can't* know the highest form of love unless you know a child as your own."

I should know. It was this death-dealing script that nearly killed me. Twice. It nearly killed me when I was childless and didn't feel *capable of* the big, exceptional love mothers talked about. And then it nearly killed me again when I became a mother and didn't *experience* the big, exceptional love mothers talked about.

Honestly, I'm now convinced that almost every shred of shame I have swallowed before and after motherhood is not because I don't love children or my children but because of the insistence that I'm supposed to *exceptionally* love them, more than anything.

More than work and dogs and books and bike rides and blood-red leaves and cotton skies.

More than friends and neighbors and parents and panhandlers.

More than Rush.

More than life.

And sometimes God, too.

Other Love

It was because of this, the mother of all scripts, that I almost counted myself out of parenting entirely. And I very well might have. Had I not met Anna.

Anna was a clinical social worker who came assigned to us shortly after we began fostering. About my age, she had an open face with a toothy grin and a stuffed hamster for a sidekick. She also sometimes, much to my delight, started sentences with "I don't know if I should be telling you this but . . ." From the moment Rush and I sat together on her saggy loveseat for our first session of therapy, we felt held. Squishy but held.

Rush and I were sitting on that same saggy loveseat when we told her, some months later, of our decision to adopt the girls. We thought the answer was "yes," we explained, but had fears, boatloads of fears.

"Like what?" Anna wanted to know, not one to settle for abstractions like *boatloads*.

"Like what if I don't enjoy it?" I asked.

"Well, what do you do for fun now?" Anna replied. "Keep doing that."

"Oh, okay," I said. This sounded logical enough to me at the time.

"So, what else?" she pried. "Give me another fear."

I looked to Rush on my right for help, but he was motionless. So, I continued on, spiraling deeper and deeper until I hit upon something in my sternum that felt like the mother of all fears.

"Well, what if I don't feel it? What if I never feel the love?" I was surprised it had come to this. My God, if anyone should know that feelings are a faulty measure of meaning, it was Catholics. And yet I had internalized—how could I not?—years of messaging that said a woman would never *know* love, *feel* love, until she became a mother.

My brain knew this was preposterous. My brain knew this, without a cobweb of doubt, and yet my heart—or was it coming from the constriction in my throat?—still wanted to know, *But what if it is true, and I am the exception to the rule?*

What if there is a mom gene, and I don't have it? What if I am defective? What if I am disastrous? What if it does matter, all my principles aside, that they are not "my own"? What if I become a parent and discover I am just as immature, unhappy, and robotic as I've ever been?

"Then you get to work," Anna said, interrupting my internal free fall. "Some loves are born of feeling. Other loves take practice. But that doesn't make them any less love and you any less worthy."

We all sat there in a moment of silence. Rush and I on the saggy loveseat. Anna on her swivel chair. It was evident something had shifted among us, and it wasn't just the leaning picture books on her shelves or the stacks of half-dressed dolls in their beach house. I wanted to stay in the certainty of that square room and never leave, but I couldn't come up with any more fears that needed airing. So, we thanked her. She nodded. And we thanked her again, our theologian in disguise.

TECHNICALLY SPEAKING, IN the Christian story, the highest form of love is not familial love but *agape* love. Agape love is not a love of passion—or deep feeling. Nor is it a love of possession—or easy belonging. It is an "other love," a love that Episcopal priest Edward Nason West deftly described as "profound concern for the well-being of another, without any desire to control that other, to be thanked by that other, or to enjoy the process."

On first listen, this "other love" may sound a lot like mother love: relentless, thankless, sometimes joyless. But I like to think of it as a bigger love, an umbrella love you could even say, to mother love. Sometimes it is even a love that runs counter to what many Americans say they like best about being parents. They want to shape their own people, choose some names, buy a house with a mantel on which to hang some oversized socks once a year. They want to be thanked and hugged and loved in return. They are looking for fulfillment, a way to give purpose to the darkling abyss that is a human life. These are not bad things to want. But this is not agape love. Agape love is what characterizes the love of God.

I know, I know, I know. There are some who will want to say that God's love *is* best pictured as a parent (though, arguably, not a biological one). How else do you explain the cornerstone Christian verse, scrawled on oversized posters at baseball games and street corners, "For God so loved the world that he gave his only Son . . ."?* Allow me, though, to point out one last textual irritant. It doesn't say that *God so loved his only Son* that God gave him to the world. It says *God so loved the world* that God privileged this "other love"

---

* One final nerdy footnote: While Father and Son language is a common way to describe the relationship between God and Jesus (and is obviously implied in John 3:16), it wasn't always a point of emphasis. The apologists of the first two centuries generally preferred to identify Jesus with the title of *Logos* from my favorite "word making world" creation story. Not until Origen's phrase, "Son of the Father," gained prominence from his treatise *De Principiis* in the early-to-middle third century did the kinship pairing take root in theological discourse and, in the fourth century, become the preferred metaphor for describing God's rich relationship with Godself and, only by extension, humanity.

over "familial love." It's a shocking, maybe even troubling, premise. But I think it's true. I think *other love* is the umbrella under which, together, we bear our best and juiciest fruit. *Other love* is how we multiply our biggest and wildest purpose. *Other love* is a democratic love that we can know and grow whether we ever partner, parent, or procreate. No one is excluded from knowing "a love like this."

Not everyone is compelled by the Christian story, of course, interpretations of which have been used mercilessly throughout history to convince people of many persuasions, but particularly women, and particularly women who refute the promise of motherhood, that they are less than fully human. I share it here at the end, not as a fat and tidy bow, but a single thread of hope: If we go looking, there are stories both major and minor, cultural and personal, ancient and new about the astonishingly good life you can live when you love and are loved as "someone other than a mother."

Until the hegemony of Mother or Mother Superior disappears, and I'm not sure that it soon will, I want to offer the phrase "someone other than a mother" as another imperfect solution that has as its aim refusal, inclusion, and resistance. We can refuse to be defined and divided by our motherhood status. We can include anyone, of any gender, who feels unseen or uninspired by maternal exceptionalism. And by leaving the word *mother* in our descriptor, we can both acknowledge and resist the material conditions that are crushing caregivers who want and need to be valued as "something other."

If the challenge is, in part, a linguistic one, then I'd like to think the answer can be worked out word by word, too. We can mind our subjects, making friends with "I" statements and choosing carefully our universals. We can learn each other's names, softening our emphasis on roles and being bare-faced human souls together. We can tell the surly, tender truths about our lives. All of us, whether mom, non-mom, or someone in between. How, sometimes, we are not as sure as we let on. How it surprises us now, our choices, our lack of choices. How we are not badasses for mothering and we are not badasses for not-mothering. Please, God, save us all from having to be badasses. We are so much *more*.

The answer isn't only in the words we choose, though. It's also in the words we collect, the words that recollect us. The books that take over our fireplace mantels. The dining room tables we lean over to listen. The lines that come to us in our head, and in notebooks, and before bed. "Make it beautiful anyway, okay?" I used to say to the dark. Now, I hear only this: "There's beauty in the making."

Beyond Before and After

July 1, 2021

Dear Self,

One last letter, this one to yourself, because you are always kinder in writing, and you are wishing this kindness upon others.

When you started, you were scared. You were scared that there was something wrong with you for not feeling what you are supposed to feel about motherhood. Before mothering, you worried that your happiness was thin. After mothering, you worried that your unhappiness was hurtful. Now, you wonder, what if there is no "before and after"?

From the moment she gets her period, if she gets her period, a woman's life is split into two. Once, her body was thought to exist mostly for itself; now it is thought capable of existing for others. She grows older and the dichotomy persists. A childless woman is thought to exist mostly for herself; a mother is thought capable of existing for others. It is a conversion formula. Once you were lost, now you are found.

Maybe it is because you don't remember your conversion, or maybe it is because you have to be daily converted that you no longer believe in hard-and-fast "befores" and "afters."

You make a list of some things you understood before mothering: that your body is a house of belonging, that your house is a home for the holy, that not giving birth can be an act of faith, too.

You make a list of some things you understood after mothering: that relationship grows capacity, that our capacity is bigger than we think, that online grocery shopping is not giving up.

It's possible you might never have known these things had you not become a mother. But you bet time, which is also to say God, would have taught them to you anyhow.

Becoming a mother is supposed to teach you a limitless love.

This is what people mean when they say, "You've never known a love like this." But you do not buy this. Becoming a mother has only reinforced for you that you are very limited, but that limits are how love multiplies. People get confused by this, you think.

Parents see their love multiplying and assume it is exclusive to them. It is not. Love multiplies whenever we take on a task that is too hard to go it alone and too worthy not to go it at all. There are limitless ways to love to your limit. You know this not because you are a mother, but because you are a grown-up.

One of the great paradoxes of being a grown-up is that as your capacity increases, so, too, does your back pain. There are other great paradoxes. You are both wiser and more uncertain. You are both softer and, about some things, more of a hard-ass. You know that it's possible to both exist for yourself and be capable of existing for others. This is the lifelong work of a life well-lived.

When you started, you were scared. You were scared that you were incapable of love. Sometimes you still get scared. It's okay. Being scared can cause you to befriend your body. (Your body is a kind of "other," too.) To slow down, put your palm to your chest, and hear your heart, in concert with the rest of the beloved community that lives within, say:

I know.

This is a lot.

But promise.

We will not abandon you here.

So be it,

Erin

Acknowledgments

ANYONE WHO'S EVER written a book knows that it is the loveliest and loneliest group project; at the end of it all, they put only your name on the cover. So, here are my unsung conspirators.

Janell and Dani, thank you for flying across the country for our Wild Woman Retreat and then listening to me read early bits of this book out loud and then wine tasting until our cheeks turned pink. I am resisting midwifery metaphors here.

The Collegeville Institute and my dreamy cohort, you saved me from making some truly foul art. I will not soon forget you, or our lunch spreads.

The Louisville Institute and its grantees, you gave me real hope (the kind backed by real money) that some pastoral leaders still care about preaching a Gospel of belonging and not body parts.

Jonathan Merritt, for being my agent through chronic doubt. I got so lucky with you. You are the best kind of bossy.

Joanna Ng and the mighty team at TarcherPerigee, for championing what this book wanted to be from the very beginning.

Lisa, Em, and Ashley, for storming heaven on my behalf with your glitter pee and rainbow GIFs.

All our social workers, therapists, educators, and extended kith and kin, thank you for making my life feel not just tolerable but wonderful sometimes.

Rush, thank you for doing 90 percent of the parenting for the last two years. We can go back now to our normal 60 percent (you), 40 percent (me) split. Girls, I may doubt the promise of motherhood, but I do not doubt you.

The privilege of talking to other women who are rewriting the mother scripts made this work infinitely less lonely and more lovely. Heaping on to those already named, thank you to Iris, Blair, Margaret, Nicholle, Alexan, Becky, lizzie, Jessica, Holly (and Andrew), Dana (and Fred), Melody, Karen, Sarah S., Shalom, Jeanette, and Jacki. Thanks, too, to my generous readers. Again, heaping on to those already named, thank you to Jenna, Emily, Tiya, Meg, Daniella, Sarah H., and Alan, and to my masterminds, Cara and Micha. Lauren, your straight talk throughout was a lifeline. I cherish when you told me, "Be quiet, so I can think."

One final note: Completing this book would not have been possible without a room in a house on some land that was home to elders, both human and non-human, before me. The ashes of my Amelia, my heart, are scattered here now. I stand in your long, motherly shadows.

Notes

1. Rebecca Solnit, *The Mother of All Questions* (New York: Haymarket Books, 2017), 10.

Preface: Mother or Mother Superior

1. Alexis Pauline Gumbs, "Introduction," in *Revolutionary Mothering: Love on the Front Lines*, ed. Alexis Pauline Gumbs, China Martens, and Mai'a Williams (Oakland, CA: PM Press, 2016), 115–16.
2. Dr. Amy Blackstone, *Childfree by Choice: The Movement Redefining Family and Creating a New Age of Independence* (New York: Dutton, 2019), 4–5.
3. Jesse Bering, "God's Little Rabbits," *Scientific American*, December 22, 2010, https://blogs.scientificamerican.com/bering-in-mind/gods-little-rabbits-religious-people-out-reproduce-secular-ones-by-a-landslide/.
4. Joyce C. Abma and Gladys M. Martinez, "Childlessness among Older Women in the United States: Trends and Profiles," *Journal of Marriage and Family* 68, no. 4 (November 1, 2006): 1055.
5. Mary K. Hunt, "On the Childfree, Religion, and Stigma Consciousness" (sociology honors thesis, University of Maine, 2015).
6. Ana C. Ribeiro, Sergei Musatov, Anna Shteyler, Serge Simanduyev, Isabel Arrieta-Cruz, Sonoko Ogawa, and Donald W. Pfaff, "SiRNA Silencing of Estrogen Receptor-α Expression Specifically in Medial Preoptic Area Neurons Abolishes Maternal Care in Female Mice," *PNAS* 109, no. 40 (October 2, 2012): https://www.pnas.org/content/109/40/16324.

Chapter 1: Your Biological Clock Is Ticking

1. Howard Thurman, "The Sound of the Genuine" (speech), Atlanta, GA, May 4, 1980, transcribed by the Crossings Project, https://uindy.edu /eip/files/reflection4.pdf.

2. C. S. Lewis, letter to Sheldon Vanauken, in Sheldon Vanauken, *A Severe Mercy* (San Francisco: HarperOne, [1977] 1980), 210.

3. The Editors of Encyclopedia Brittanica, "Curt Paul Richter," *Encyclopedia Brittanica*, last modified February 16, 2021, https://www .britannica.com/biography/curt-paul-richter#ref276214.

4. Richard Cohen, "The Clock Is Ticking for the Career Woman," *The Washington Post*, March 16, 1978, https://www.washingtonpost.com /archive/local/1978/03/16/the-clock-is-ticking-for-the-career -woman/bd566aa8-fd7d-43da-9be9-ad025759d0a4/.

5. William Goode, as quoted by Betty Rollin in "Motherhood: Who Needs It," *Look* (September 22, 1970): http://jackiewhiting.net/collab /exploratory/motherhood.htm.

6. Gary Brase and Sandra Brase, "Emotional Regulation of Fertility Decision Making: What Is the Nature and Structure of 'Baby Fever'?," *Emotion* 12, no. 5 (August 2011): 1141–54, https://doi.org/10.1037/a0024954.

7. Gabrielle Moss, "Why Women's 'Biological Clock Ticking' Is Actually a Total Myth," *Bustle*, March 8, 2016, https://www.bustle.com/articles /146600-why-womens-biological-clock-ticking-is-actually-a-total-myth.

8. Candida R. Moss and Joel S. Baden, *Reconceiving Infertility: Biblical Perspectives on Procreation & Childlessness* (Princeton, NJ: Princeton University Press, 2015), 80.

9. Dianne Hales, *Just Like a Woman: How Gender Science Is Redefining What Makes Us Female* (New York: Bantam, 1999), 173.

10. Miranda Gray, *Red Moon* (United Kingdom: Fastprint Gold, 2009), location 1302–16, Kindle.

11. Thurman, "The Sound of the Genuine."

Chapter 2: Home Is Your Highest Duty

1. Alice Walker, "Desire," in *The World Will Follow Joy: Turning Madness into Flowers* (New York: The New Press, 2013), 78.

2. Theodore Roosevelt, "Speech to the National Congress of Mothers," March 9, 1905, in *Report of the National Congress of Mothers*, vol. 9 (1905).

3. Frederic Schoff, "The National Congress of Mothers and Parent-Teacher Associations," *The Annals of the American Academy of Political Science*, vol. 67, *New Possibilities in Education* (September 1916): 141–42.

4. Roosevelt, "Speech to the National Congress of Mothers."

5. Stephanie Coontz, *The Way We Never Were: American Families and the Nostalgia Trap* (New York: Basic Books, 1992), 50.

6. "Fertility of Women in the United States," United States Census Bureau, last updated April 3, 2019, https://www.census.gov/data/tables/2018/demo/fertility/women-fertility.html#par_list_57.

7. Lauren Sandler, "Having It All Without Having Children," *Time*, August 12, 2013, http://content.time.com/time/subscriber/article/0,33009,2148636-1,00.html.

8. Char Williams, "Being a Black Woman Who Doesn't Want Kids Means Twice the Judgement," *Bustle*, February 27, 2017, https://www.bustle.com/p/being-a-black-woman-who-doesnt-want-kids-means-twice-the-judgement-40988.

9. Christine Woyshner, *The National PTA, Race, and Civic Engagement, 1897–1970* (Columbus: Ohio State University Press, 2009), 31–32.

Chapter 3: Motherhood Is the Toughest Job

1. Abraham Joshua Heschel, *The Sabbath: Its Meaning for Modern Man* (New York: Farrar, Straus and Giroux, 1951), 26, Kindle.

2. Jennifer Senior, *All Joy and No Fun: The Paradox of Modern Parenting* (New York: HarperCollins, 2014), 9.

3. Katharine Lane Antolini, *Memorializing Motherhood: Anna Jarvis and the Struggle for the Control of Mother's Day* (Morgantown, WV: West Virgina University Press, 2014), 66.

4. Brigid Schulte, interview with Rebecca J. Rosen, "America's Workers: Stressed Out, Overwhelmed, Totally Exhausted," *The Atlantic*, March 25, 2015, https://www.theatlantic.com/business/archive/2014/03/americas-workers-stressed-out-overwhelmed-totally-exhausted/284615/.

5. "How Do Mothers Spend Their Time at Home?," Pew Research Forum, April 8, 2014, https://www.pewresearch.org/social-trends/2014/04/08/chapter-3-how-do-mothers-spend-their-time-at-home/.

6. Brigid Schulte, *Overwhelmed: Work, Love, and Play When No One Has the Time* (New York: Farrar, Straus and Giroux, 2014), 32.

7. "8 Facts about American Dads," Pew Research Forum, June 12, 2019, https://www.pewresearch.org/fact-tank/2019/06/12/fathers-day-facts/.

8. Jeffrey Klein, interview with Stewart D. Friedman, *Knowledge @ Wharton*, podcast transcript, October 31, 2013, https://knowledge .wharton.upenn.edu/article/stew-friedman-new-work-family-choices -men-women/.

9. Oprah Winfrey, interview with Lacey Rose, "Oprah Winfrey on Forgoing Motherhood, Being 'Counted Out' and the Meeting That Turned OWN Around," *Hollywood Reporter*, December 11, 2013, https://www.hollywoodreporter.com/tv/tv-news/oprah-winfrey -forgoing-motherhood-being-664550/.

10. Klein, interview with Stewart D. Friedman.

11. Kathryn M. Rizzo, Holly H. Schiffrin, and Miriam Liss, "Insight into the Parenting Paradox: Mental Health Outcomes of Intensive Mothering," *Journal of Child and Family Studies* 22 (July 2013): 614–20, https://doi.org/10.1007/s10826-012-9615-z.

12. Heschel, *The Sabbath*, 26.

13. "8 Facts about American Dads," Pew Research Forum.

Chapter 4: But You'd Make a Great Mom

1. Gloria Steinem, "Mother as a Verb," Women's Media Center, May 14, 2007, https://www.womensmediacenter.com/news-features/mother-as-a-verb.

2. Kate Bowler, *The Preacher's Wife: The Precarious Power of Evangelical Celebrities* (Princeton, NJ: Princeton University Press, 2019), 243.

3. Margaret Moers Wenig, "Male and Female God Created Them: Parashat Bereshit (Genesis 1:1–6:8)," in *Torah Queeries: Weekly Commentaries on the Hebrew Bible*, ed. Gregg Drinkwater, Joshua Lesser, and David Schneer (New York: NYU Press, 2009).

4. Martin Luther, *Luther's Works, Volume 1: Genesis Chapters 1–5* (St. Louis, MO: Concordia Publishing House, 2004), 199.

5. Alexis Pauline Gumbs, "m/other ourselves: a Black queer feminist genealogy for radical mothering," in *Revolutionary Mothering: Love on the Front Lines*, ed. Alexis Pauline Gumbs, China Martens, and Mai'a Williams (Oakland, CA: PM Press, 2016), 23.

6. Jessica Slice, "Imposter Syndrome and Parenting with a Disability," in *Disability Visibility: First-Person Stories from the Twenty-First Century*, ed. Alice Wong (New York: Vintage, 2020), 132.

Chapter 5: Children Are a Gift from God

1. Sheldon Vanauken, *A Severe Mercy* (San Francisco: HarperOne, [1977] 1980), 37.
2. Pope Francis, "Three Loves for One Wedding" (sermon, Domus Sanctae Marthae, Vatican City, June 2, 2014), Vatican, https://www.vatican.va /content/francesco/en/cotidie/2014/documents/papa-francesco -cotidie_20140602_three-loves.html.
3. Dale B. Martin, *Sex and the Single Savior: Gender and Sexuality in Biblical Interpretation* (Louisville, KY: Westminster John Knox Press, 2006), 106.
4. Sharyn Dowd, "1 Peter," in *Women's Bible Commentary,* ed. Carol A. Newsom and Sharon H. Ringe (Louisville, KY: Westminster John Knox Press, 1998), 463.
5. Paul VI, "Humanae Vitae" (encyclical letter), July 25, 1968, http://www.vatican.va/content/paul-vi/en/encyclicals/documents /hf_p-vi_enc_25071968_humanae-vitae.html.
6. William D. Mosher, Jo Jones, and Joyce C. Abma, "Intended and Unintended Births in the United States: 1982–2010," National Health Statistics Report, no. 55 (July 24, 2012): https://www.cdc.gov/nchs /data/nhsr/nhsr055.pdf.
7. C. S. Lewis, *The Abolition of Man* (Oxford: Oxford University Press, 1943), 17.
8. Lewis, *The Abolition of Man,* 17.
9. Vanauken, *A Severe Mercy,* 37.
10. C. S. Lewis, letter to Sheldon Vanauken, in Vanauken, *A Severe Mercy,* 209.
11. Lewis, letter to Vanauken, in Vanauken, *A Severe Mercy,* 209.
12. Dr. Amy Blackstone, *Childfree by Choice: The Movement Redefining Family and Creating a New Age of Independence* (New York: Dutton, 2019), 198.
13. Blackstone, *Childfree by Choice,* 119.
14. Ranae J. Evenson and Robin W. Simon, "Clarifying the Relationship between Parenthood and Depression," *Journal of Health and Social Behavior* 46, no. 4 (2005): 341–58.
15. General Assembly of the United Presbyterian Church in the United States of America, "Sexuality and the Human Condition" (1970): 20.
16. Katharine Jefferts Schori, interview by Deborah Solomon, "State of the Church," *The New York Times,* November 19, 2016, https://www .nytimes.com/2006/11/19/magazine/19WWLN_Q4.html.

17. Central Conference of American Rabbis, "CCAR Resolution Affirming Our Commitment to Women's Rights," March 19, 2017, https://www .ccarnet.org/ccar-resolutions/affirming-our-commitment-womens -rights/.

Chapter 6: It'll Be Different with Your Own

1. Robin Wall Kimmerer, *Braiding Sweetgrass: Indigenous Wisdom, Scientific Knowledge, and the Teachings of Plants* (Minneapolis, MN: Milkweed Editions, 2013), 97.
2. Kimmerer, *Braiding Sweetgrass*, 15.
3. Dale B. Martin, *Sex and the Single Savior: Gender and Sexuality in Biblical Interpretation* (Louisville, KY: Westminster John Knox Press, 2006), 104.
4. John Bowlby, *Maternal Care and Mental Health* (Geneva, Switzerland: World Health Organization, 1952), 35.
5. "Maternal Deprivation," in *Essential Psychology*, 2nd ed., ed. Robert Burns (Dordrecht, the Netherlands: Springer, 2008), 148.
6. Mia Birdsong, as quoted by David Brooks, "The Nuclear Family Was a Mistake," *The Atlantic*, March 2020, https://www.theatlantic.com /magazine/archive/2020/03/the-nuclear-family-was-a-mistake /605536/.
7. Bruce Perry, as quoted by Deborah Blum, *Love at Goon Park: Harry Harlow and the Science of Affection* (Cambridge, MA: Perseus Books, 2002), 287.
8. Aminatou Sow and Ann Friedman, *Big Friendship: How We Keep Each Other Close* (New York: Simon & Schuster, 2020), 45.
9. Barbara Melosh, *Strangers and Kin: The American Way of Adoption* (Cambridge, MA: Harvard University Press, 2002), 10.
10. Alison Gopnik, *Philosophical Baby: What Children's Minds Tell Us about Truth, Love, and the Meaning of Life* (New York: Picador, 2010), 243.

Chapter 7: You'll Regret Not Having Kids

1. Clarissa Pinkola Estés, *Women Who Run with the Wolves: Myths and Stories of the Wild Woman Archetype* (New York: Ballantine Books, [1992] 1995), 394.

2. May Sarton, "Now I Become Myself," *Collected Poems: 1930–1993* (New York: W. W. Norton & Company, 1993), 162.

3. Jennifer Senior, *All Joy and No Fun: The Paradox of Modern Parenting* (New York: HarperCollins, 2014), 10.

4. Andy Tower, Matt N. Williams, Stephen R. Hill, Michael C. Philipp, and Ross Flett, "What Makes for the Most Intense Regrets?," *Frontier Psychology* (December 15, 2016): https://doi.org/10.3389 /fpsyg.2016.01941.

5. "Health Survey for England, 2016," National Health Service, December 13, 2017, https://digital.nhs.uk/data-and-information/publications /statistical/health-survey-for-england/health-survey-for-england-2016.

6. Eric Klinenberg, as quoted by Lauren Sandler, "Having It All Without Having Children," *Time*, August 12, 2013, http://content.time.com /time/subscriber/article/0,33009,2148636-1,00.html.

7. Julie Ann McMullin and Victor W. Marshall, "Friends, Family, Stress, and Well-Being: Does Childlessness Make a Difference?," *Canadian Journal on Aging* 15, no. 3 (1996): 355–73.

8. Ann Crittenden, *The Price of Motherhood: Why the Most Important Job Is Still the Least Valued* (New York: Henry Holt and Company, 2001), 6.

9. Parker J. Palmer, "The Clearness Committee: A Communal Approach to Discernment," Center for Courage & Renewal, http://www .couragerenewal.org/pdfs/parker-palmer_clearness-committee.pdf.

10. Denise Lervtov, "A Gift," in *Sands of the Well* (New York: New Directions, 1996).

11. Gail Cornwall, "The Two Reasons Parents Regret Having Kids," *The Atlantic*, August 31, 2021, https://www.theatlantic.com/family /archive/2021/08/why-parents-regret-children/619931/.

12. Tomas Tranströmer, "The Blue House," trans. Samuel Charters, in *Tomas Tranströmer: Selected Poems 1954–1986*, ed. Robert Hass (New York: HarperCollins, 1987), 166.

Chapter 8: Family Is the Greatest Legacy

1. John 15:16, NRSV.

2. Candida R. Moss and Joel S. Baden, *Reconceiving Infertility: Biblical Perspectives on Procreation & Childlessness* (Princeton, NJ: Princeton University Press, 2015), 29.

3. Jennifer Senior, *All Joy and No Fun: The Paradox of Modern Parenting* (New York: HarperCollins, 2014), 5–6.

4. "As Marriage and Parenthood Drift Apart, Public Is Concerned about Social Impact," Pew Research Forum, July 1, 2007, https://www.pewresearch.org/social-trends/2007/07/01/as-marriage-and-parenthood-drift-apart-public-is-concerned-about-social-impact/.

5. Audre Lorde, *Sister Outsider: Essays and Speeches* (Berkeley, CA: Crossing Press, 1984), 173.

Chapter 9: You Don't Know Love Until You Become a Mother

1. Edward Nason West, quoted in Madeleine L'Engle, *A Circle of Quiet: The Crosswicks Journal, Book 1* (San Francisco: HarperOne, 1984), 94–95, Kindle.

2. Carolyn G. Heilbrun, *Writing a Woman's Life* (New York: Ballantine Books, 1989), 20–21.

3. Rebecca Solnit, *The Mother of All Questions* (New York: Haymarket Books, 2017), 9.

4. Julian of Norwich, *Revelations of Divine Love*, trans. Elizabeth Spearing (New York: Penguin, 1998).

5. Jessica Grose, "America's Mothers Are in Crisis," *The New York Times*, February 4, 2021, https://www.nytimes.com/2021/02/04/parenting/working-moms-mental-health-coronavirus.html.

6. Grose, "America's Mothers Are in Crisis."

7. Grose, "America's Mothers Are in Crisis."

8. Kamala Harris, "Speech at Biden/Harris Event," Wilmington, DE, August 12, 2020.

9. Alisha Haridasani Gupta, "The Suffragists Fought to Redefine Femininity. The Debate Isn't Over," *The New York Times*, August 29, 2020, https://www.nytimes.com/2020/08/26/us/womens-suffrage-femininity.html.

10. Amanda Taub, "Mothers' Power in U.S. Protests Echoes a Global Tradition," *The New York Times*, July 25, 2020, https://www.nytimes.com/2020/07/25/world/americas/protest-moms-power-police.html.

About the Author

Erin S. Lane is a writer, theologian, and someone other than a mother. She is most recently the author of *Lessons in Belonging from a Church-Going Commitment Phobe*. She holds a bachelor's degree from Davidson College and a master's degree from Duke Divinity School, both with a focus in gender studies. Mentored by Parker J. Palmer and the Center for Courage & Renewal, she works as a vocational retreat facilitator, helping people discern their wildest questions of purpose. She resides in Raleigh, North Carolina, with her improbable kin.